D1806186
9780562000274

Photography: John Lee Studio
                Roy Rich, Angel Studio
                Christian Delu

© Copyright 1975 Purnell & Sons Ltd.
Published 1975 by Sampson Low, Berkshire House,
Queen Street, Maidenhead, Berkshire.
Printed in Italy.
SBN 562 00027 5

Four Seasons Cookery Books

Autumn

Audrey Ellis

Drawings by Marilyn Day

Sampson Low

Contents

Useful information

Metric measures: The new standard measure holds 3 dl. (300 ml.) which is just under ½ pint.

1. Sets of metric spoons are available now in the following capacities:— 15 ml. (1 tablespoon), 10 ml., 5 ml. (1 teaspoon), 2.5 ml. The full set comprises two additional spoons, 20 ml. and 1.25 ml. but these are optional. To avoid confusion with earlier (Imperial) standard equipment and existing domestic cutlery, the term 'cup' will be replaced by 'measure' and spoons will eventually be referred to by capacity rather than tablespoon and teaspoon.

2. The new metric measuring jugs contain 1 litre, or ½ litre. The litre jug is marked at 7.5 dl., ½ litre/5 dl., 1.5 dl. and 1 dl.

3. The metric unit of weight is the kilogram (kg.) which is 1000 g. or 2.2 lb. Where recipes give ingredients in ounces, the metric unit of 25 g. has been found practical. Spring balance scales marked in metric or dual-marked in metric and Imperial are available. The pointer shows 1 kilo/2¼ lbs. and indicates divisions of 500 g./18 oz., 250 g./9 oz. and 125 g./4½ oz. Smaller units are marked at intervals of 25 g. Most food packs show weights in both systems, e.g. 4 oz. (113 g.) or 500 g. (1 lb. 1½ oz.).

Oven temperature chart

	°F	°C	Gas Mark
Very cool	225	110	¼
	250	130	½
Cool	275	140	1
	300	150	2
Moderate	325	170	3
	350	180	4
Moderately hot	375	190	5
	400	200	6
Hot	425	220	7
	450	230	8
Very hot	475	240	9

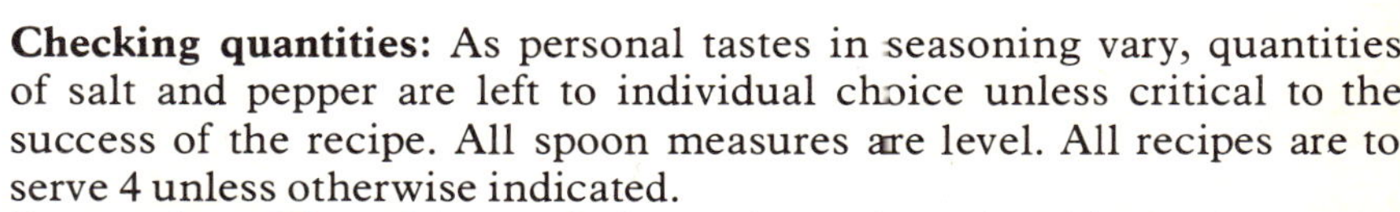

Checking quantities: As personal tastes in seasoning vary, quantities of salt and pepper are left to individual choice unless critical to the success of the recipe. All spoon measures are level. All recipes are to serve 4 unless otherwise indicated.

Seasonal cooking: Many of the recipes given in this book can be used in other seasons. For example there is a summer season for avocados and a winter season. Some items are constantly available frozen or canned.

Acknowledgments

The author and publishers thank the following for their help in supplying photographs for this book

Olives From Spain, p. 22
The Apple and Pear Development Council, p. 20, p. 24, p. 44
British Sugar Bureau, p. 23, p. 70
The U.S. Rice Council, p. 19
The Pasta Information Centre, p. 31
Culpeper Herbs and Spices, p. 27
Hassy Perfection Celery, p. 33
Gale's Honey, p. 32
Pyroflam by James A. Jobling, Ltd., p. 36
Colman's Mustard, p. 37
California Wine Institute, p. 40
New Zealand Lamb Information Bureau, p. 38
Buxted Brand Products by Ross Poultry Ltd., p. 42, p. 76
James Robertson & Sons (Preserve Manufacturers) Ltd., p. 43
John West Foods, p. 45, p. 59, p. 64
Baxters of Speyside, p. 48
The Tupperware Company, p. 69
The Carnation Milk Bureau, p. 67
The National Dairy Council, p. 66
Alcan Polyfoil Ltd., p. 78

Introduction

Autumn brings to our kitchens the richest bounty of the year . . . a time when baskets are abrim with luscious fruit and vegetables. It is by tradition the mellow, misty season for preserving and putting its glorious harvest into store. There is so much to choose from, both for immediate use or to be carefully packed and arranged in attic, barn and freezer. Onions hanging by the plait, apples and pears spaced well apart on slatted shelves, make a pleasant and comforting sight as winter approaches. So do stacks of frozen containers marked 'Tomato curd', or 'Cream of pumpkin soup'.

Cook for today, store and freeze for tomorrow, using the recipes in this book which have been created to make the fullest use possible of autumnal delights. My intention, as you will see, is not to linger over basic cookery methods probably already familiar; rather to introduce original ideas which will contribute many future favourites to your repertoire of recipes.

The buying guide for this time of year is crowded with succulent items. It's the season when vegetables come in all shapes and gorgeous colours and game arrives on the scene to make a rich alternative to delicate poultry dishes.

There is a re-awakening interest in the art of making bread at home. Because the harvest festival conjures up visions of crusty loaves as well as giant marrows, this is the season in which I have chosen to include a section on bread. I do hope you try baking a few small loaves in earthenware flower pots and enjoy as I do the good smell of yeast dough, so evocative of a cosy farmhouse kitchen.

Then come my recipes for meals, divided into groups; simple dishes for everyday and more sophisticated ones for entertaining, as indicated below. All have one thing in common, they make use of fresh produce at the peak of availability or simply suit the time of year.

Pickles and preserves are fun to make, and a natural choice for Autumn, especially the rather unusual ones I have devised for you. Fortunate freezer owners already know that this is when vegetables tempt them most to fill up with a year's supply.

For a spectacular finish, there is a plan complete with recipes for a romantic candlelight buffet party—an attractive thought at this time when the days draw in so early and the first nip comes in the air.

It is my sincere hope that this book will bring a touch of inspiration to your menu plans this and every Autumn.

 Sophisticated

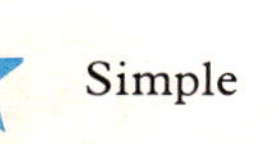 Simple

Buying guide for the season

Your Autumn purchases need extra planning according to the space and facilities you have available for storage. If a freezer is not on your list of domestic equipment, study the best ways to pack. It pays to know when you are likely to buy the produce of these three months at a rock bottom price because a glut is likely to occur. Also, how to judge its quality.

Hard fruit picked from a tree can be separately wrapped and stored in a fairly cold but *dry* atmosphere in boxes. If unwrapped, spaced well apart so that no one fruit touches another, on shelves (preferably slatted shelves to allow circulation of air). Apples and pears are the obvious candidates. Do not attempt to store any that are bruised or have brownish patches—this applies to both dessert and cooking varieties. Use damaged fruit for jams and purées. The fruit should be hard to the touch and very slightly under-ripe as it matures further during storage. For immediate eating pears especially are better bought just before the peak of ripeness, for in a warm atmosphere they soon get 'sleepy' (soft around the core) and if they require to be brought on quickly put them in the airing cupboard or other warm place for one or two days.

Storing root vegetables will be dealt with in the Winter volume, but both tomatoes and onions are ready to store during the Autumn months. Tomatoes are in fact a fruit and if picked under-ripe, even slightly tinged with orange, will usually ripen fully in the course of a few weeks. They should be separately wrapped in paper and packed without pressure in boxes or a deep drawer as for apples, but require to be sorted through and any which have gone soft to be removed frequently. Green tomatoes of course are not a dead loss as they make excellent preserves and pickles and taste delicious sliced in half and fried or grilled for breakfast. Onions tend to sprout if left in a damp place, but I find the method which preserves them longest is to plait, starting with three strands of raffia tied at one end, and weaving in the dried onion tops as you go. Long onion plaits should be hung up and onions snipped off for use, reserving the best preserved ones until the last. Use up quickly any that show signs of fresh growth.

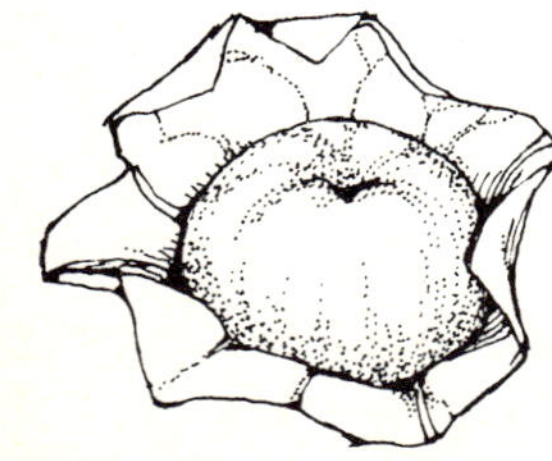

Autumn — early

Fish	**Meat, Poultry and game**	**Fruit**	**Vegetables**
Bream	Duck	Apples	Aubergines
Crab	Goose	Bilberries	Avocado pears
Dabs	Grouse	Blackberries	Beetroots
Dover sole	Guinea fowl	Blueberries	Broccoli
Eels	Hare	Charentais	(white/green)
Grey mullet	Partridge	melons	Brussels sprouts
Hake	Pigeon	Chinese	Carrots
Halibut	Rabbit	gooseberries	Cauliflower
Herring	Quail	Damsons	Celeriac
Lemon sole	Scotch beef	Figs	Celery
Lobster	Scotch lamb	Grapes	Corn on the cob
Mackerel	Snipe	Greengages	Courgettes
Mock halibut	Teal	Honeydew melons	Field mushrooms
Mussels	Turkey	Lemons	Horseradish
Portuguese	Venison	Loganberries	Leeks
oysters	Welsh lamb	Ogen melons	Lettuce
Prawns	Wild duck	Peaches	Marrows
Rainbow trout		Pears	Onions
Red mullet		Plums	Radishes
Salmon		Pomegranates	Savoy cabbage
Sea trout		Raspberries	Shallots
Shrimps		(second crop)	Spinach
Turbot		Strawberries	Swedes
Whiting		(second crop)	Turnips
Witch		Watermelons	

Autumn — late

Fish	**Meat, Poultry and game**	**Fruit**	**Vegetables**
Bass	Duck	Apples	Aubergines
Bream	English beef	Chinese	Avocados
Brill	Goose	gooseberries	Beetroot
Carp	Hare	Clementines	Broccoli
Clams	Mallard	Coconuts	Brussels sprouts
Cod	Partridge	Cranberries	Celery
Conger eels	Pheasant	Dates	Celeriac
Eels	Pigeon	Grapes	Chicory
Haddock	Quail	Lemons	Corn on the cob
Hake	Rabbit	Limes	Endive
Halibut	Scotch beef	Mandarines	Fennel
Herring	Scotch lamb	Mangoes	Globe
Lemon sole	Snipe	Medlars	artichokes
Mussels	Teal	Nectarines	Jerusalem
Plaice	Turkey	Pawpaws	artichokes
Rock salmon	Venison	Pears	Leeks
Scallops	Wild goose	Pomegranates	Onions
Skate	Woodcock	Satsumas	Parsley
Sprats		Spanish oranges	Parsnips
Turbot	Nuts:	Tangerines	Potatoes
Whitebait	Almonds	Ugli fruits	Swedes
Winkles	Brazil nuts		Turnips
	Chestnuts		
	Filberts		
	Walnuts		

Certain items such as mushrooms, bananas, chicken, etc. are omitted as they are available from various sources throughout the year with little variation in price.

Varieties to choose

Home-grown dessert apples: Worcester Pearmain, pale green flushing to crimson—September to November (stores well). Egremont Russet, bronze with a matt pale brown surface—October to December. Cox's Orange Pippin, golden yellow streaked to light red and flushing to brick red—September to May. Laxton's Fortune, sharp green streaked with crimson and flushing to bright crimson—September to October. James Grieve, greenish yellow and pale yellow with orange red flush and stripes—September to October. Laxton's Superb, yellowish green to pale lemon yellow, usually much flushed and streaked dull red with a little russet—November onwards. Beauty of Bath, greenish to yellow orange, striped or spotted red with network of russet—early August. Ellison's Orange, greenish yellow to yellow with many red streaks and flecks—October.

Imported dessert apples: Golden Delicious, pale green turning to pale yellow—September onwards.

Home-grown cooking apples: Bramley's Seedling—October onwards. Lord Derby—July onwards. Grenadier—August/September. Crab apples are home grown and not often available in shops—September to October.

Home-grown dessert pears: Conference, long tapering shape, mid green with bronze spots—October to November (stores well). Doyenne du Comice, large oval shape, pale yellow flushing to red or russet—October to December (store until March). William bon Chrétien (Bartlett), large medium pale green changing to clear yellow with faint russet—August to September. Dr. Jules Guyot, large greenish yellow, turning clear pale yellow, slightly flushed—September. Beurre Hardy, large yellowy green thickly russeted—September to October.

Home-grown cooking pears: Pitmaston Duchesse, nearly round with tough yellow to green skin, irregularly spotted with russet—October to December.

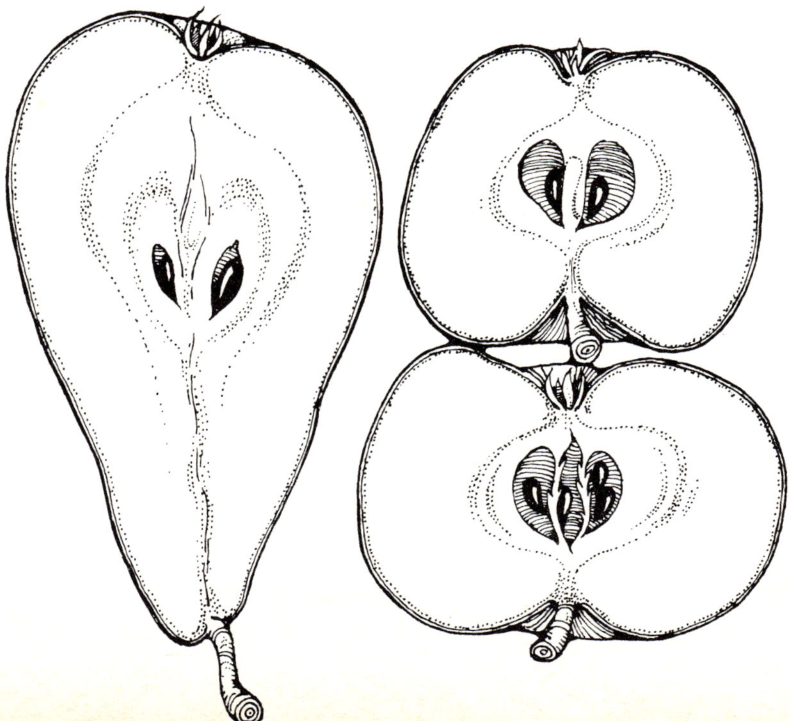

Harvest time — How to make bread

Flour is quite heavy to handle in bulk but a batch of bread made with three pounds is manageable. Here are basic recipes for plain white, enriched and wholewheat doughs, each with variations.

Basic white bread chain

Imperial/Metric
2 teaspoons sugar
½ pint/3 dl. warm water
1 oz./25 g. dried yeast or
2 oz./50 g. fresh yeast
3 oz./75 g. margarine
1 pint/generous ½ litre
hot water
1 tablespoon salt
3 lb./1½ kg. strong plain
flour

American
2 teaspoons sugar
1¼ cups warm water
2½ tablespoons dried yeast
or I cake compressed
yeast
⅓ cup margarine
2½ cups hot water
1 tablespoon salt
12 cups all-purpose flour

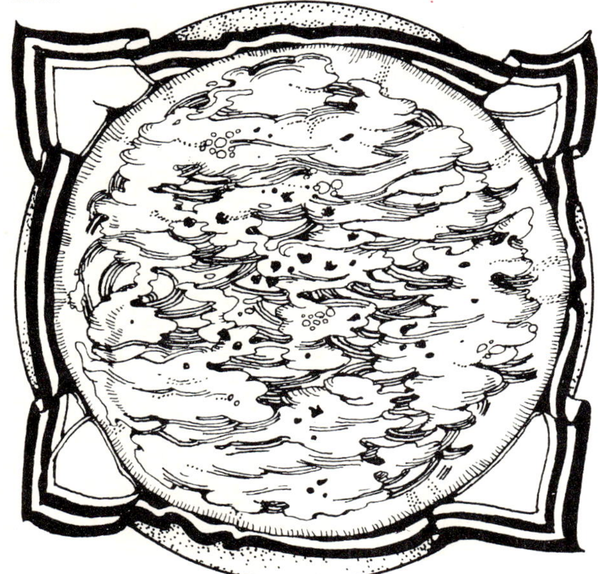

Dissolve the sugar in the warm water and sprinkle in the yeast. Leave in a warm place until frothy, about 10 minutes. Melt the margarine in the hot water, stir in the salt and cool to lukewarm. Add a little of the flour and beat for 2 minutes. Add the yeast liquid and sufficient flour to make a stiff dough. Turn out on a lightly floured board and knead until the dough is smooth and elastic, about 10 minutes. Shape the dough into a ball and place in a greased bowl. Cover with a damp cloth (or slip it into a greased polythene bag) and let rise in a warm place until doubled in bulk, about one hour. Turn out and knead lightly. Divide into three.

Sandwich loaf: Shape one third of the dough into a loaf and place in a greased 2 lb./1 kg. loaf tin. Cover and let rise until double in bulk, about 40 minutes. Bake in a hot oven (425°F, 220°C, Gas Mark 7) for 10 minutes, then bake in a moderately hot oven (375°F, 190°C, Gas Mark 5) for 40 minutes or until the loaf sounds hollow when tapped. Turn out immediately and let cool on a wire rack.

Cottage loaf Shape another portion of the dough into one large ball and one smaller ball. Place the large ball on a greased baking tray and place the smaller ball on top. Push the handle of a wooden spoon through the centre of the dough, through to the baking tray. Let the cottage loaf rise in a warm place until doubled in bulk. Follow the baking directions above.

Pizzas with Mozzarella

Imperial/Metric
1 lb./½ kg. tomatoes
8 oz./225 g. Mozzarella
cheese
1 teaspoon dried oregano
salt and pepper
3 tablespoons olive oil

American
1 lb. tomatoes
½ lb. Mozzarella cheese
1 teaspoon dried oregano
salt and pepper
3 tablespoons olive oil

Use the remaining dough to make pizzas. Roll to ¼ inch/6 mm. thickness. Cut the dough into 12 circles and place on greased baking trays. Slice the tomatoes and Mozzarella cheese thinly. Cover each dough circle with a layer of tomatoes and cheese. Sprinkle with oregano, salt and pepper. Add another layer of tomatoes and cheese and brush the oil over each pizza. Bake in a moderately hot oven (400°F, 200°C, Gas Mark 6) for 25-30 minutes.

Enriched white bread chain

Imperial/Metric
1 oz./25 g. dried yeast or
  2 oz./50 g. fresh yeast
$\frac{1}{4}$ pint/1$\frac{1}{2}$ dl. warm water
3 lb./1$\frac{1}{2}$ kg. strong plain
  flour
$\frac{3}{4}$ pint/4 dl. milk
5 oz./150 g. margarine
2 teaspoons malt extract
1 tablespoon salt
2 eggs

American
2$\frac{1}{2}$ tablespoons dried yeast
  or 1 cake compressed
  yeast
$\frac{2}{3}$ cup warm water
12 cups all-purpose flour
2 cups milk
$\frac{2}{3}$ cup margarine
2 teaspoons malt extract
1 tablespoon salt
2 eggs

Dissolve the yeast in the warm water and beat in 8 oz./225 g. flour. Cover with a damp cloth and let rise for 30 minutes. Scald the milk; add the margarine, malt and salt. Cool to lukewarm. Beat the eggs lightly and add to the sponge. Then beat in the scalded milk mixture and the remaining flour. Mix with the hand until it forms a soft, but not sticky dough. Cover with a damp cloth and let rise in a warm place until doubled in bulk, about 1 hour. Divide the dough into three.

Poppy seed plait: You will require one beaten egg to glaze and 2 tablespoons poppy seed. On a floured board, roll one piece of the dough into three long strips. Plait the three strips of dough together on a greased baking tray. Let double in bulk. Brush with beaten egg and sprinkle with poppy seeds. Bake in a hot oven (425°F, 220°C, Gas Mark 7) for 10 minutes, then lower heat to moderately hot (400°F, 200°C, Gas Mark 6) for 25 minutes. Cool on a wire rack.

Hungarian bubble loaf

Imperial/Metric
4 oz./125 g. butter, melted
2 oz./50 g. soft brown
  sugar
2 teaspoons ground
  cinnamon
2 oz./50 g. chopped
  walnuts
2 oz./50 g. glacé cherries

American
$\frac{1}{2}$ cup melted butter
$\frac{1}{4}$ cup light brown sugar
2 teaspoons ground
  cinnamon
$\frac{1}{2}$ cup chopped walnuts
$\frac{1}{2}$ cup candied cherries

Roll another third of the dough into small balls. Dip each ball in the melted butter, then roll in a mixture of the sugar and cinnamon. Place a layer of coated balls in a buttered 9 inch/23 cm. ring cake tin. Scatter a few chopped nuts and cherries on top. Alternate layers of coated dough balls, nuts and cherries until half the tin is filled. Cover and let rise in a warm place until the dough reaches the top of the tin. Bake in a moderately hot oven (400°F, 200°C, Gas Mark 6) for 10 minutes, then reduce oven temperature to 375°F, 190°C, Gas Mark 5 and bake 20-25 minutes longer. Cool on a wire rack.

Cheese herb buffet loaves

Imperial/Metric
2 oz./50 g. grated
  Parmesan cheese
2 oz./50 g. finely chopped
  parsley
$\frac{1}{2}$ teaspoon dried oregano
$\frac{1}{2}$ teaspoon garlic salt
beaten egg to glaze
2 tablespoons sesame seeds

American
$\frac{1}{2}$ cup grated Parmesan
  cheese
$\frac{1}{2}$ cup finely chopped
  parsley
$\frac{1}{2}$ teaspoon dried
  oregano
$\frac{1}{2}$ teaspoon garlic salt
beaten egg to glaze
2 tablespoons sesame seeds

Roll the remaining dough into two 9 inch/23 cm. ×12 inch/30 cm. rectangles. Mix cheese, parsley, oregano and garlic salt. Sprinkle evenly over each rectangle. Tightly roll up and place seam side down on two greased baking trays. Cover and let rise in a warm place until double in bulk. Brush with beaten egg and sprinkle with sesame seeds. Follow the baking directions for Hungarian bubble loaf.

Wholewheat bread chain

Imperial/Metric
4 tablespoons dried yeast
  or 1½ oz./40 g. fresh
  yeast
¾ pint/4 dl. warm water
1¼ pints/¾ litre milk
4 oz./125 g. margarine
¼ pint/1½ dl. treacle
1½ tablespoons salt
3 lb./1½ kg. wholewheat
  flour
3 tablespoons wheat germ

American
4 tablespoons dried yeast
  or 1½ cakes compressed
  yeast
2 cups warm water
3 cups milk
½ cup shortening
⅔ cup molasses
1½ tablespoons salt
12½ cups wholewheat flour
3 tablespoons wheat germ

Dissolve the yeast in the warm water and set in a warm place until frothy. Scald the milk; add the margarine, treacle, and salt. Cool to lukewarm. Beat in 8 oz./225 g. flour and the wheat germ. Beat for two minutes. Stir in the yeast liquid and sufficient flour to make a stiff dough. Turn out on a lightly floured board and knead until the dough is smooth and elastic, about 10 minutes. Place in a greased bowl, cover with a damp cloth and let rise until doubled in bulk, about 1 hour. Divide the dough into three.

Round cob: Shape one third of the dough into a round and place on a greased baking sheet. Cover and let rise in a warm place until almost doubled. Bake in a moderately hot oven (400°F, 200°C, Gas Mark 6) for 10 minutes, then lower heat to moderate (350°F, 180°C, Gas Mark 4) for 30 minutes. Brush loaf with warmed honey and let cool on a wire rack.

Flower-pot loaves: Shape another third of the dough into three balls. Place each ball in a well greased earthenware pot measuring 5 inches/13 cm. diameter at the top. (The flower pots should be seasoned before using by greasing well and then baked in a hot oven (425°F, 220°C, Gas Mark 7) for 30 minutes.) Brush the top of the dough with salt and water and sprinkle with cracked wheat. Cover and let rise in a warm place until the dough reaches the top of the pots. Bake in a hot oven (425°F, 220°C, Gas Mark 7) for 30 minutes.

Shape the remaining dough into plain or fancy rolls.

Parkerhouse rolls: On a lightly floured board, roll out dough to ¼ inch/6 mm. thickness. Cut into 2½ inch/6 cm. circles. Brush melted butter to within ¼ inch/ 6 mm. of the edges of each circle, fold the circles in half and pinch the edges together to seal. Place on greased baking trays. Cover and let rise until doubled. Brush with beaten egg and sprinkle with caraway seeds. Bake in a moderately hot oven (400°F, 200°C, Gas Mark 6) for 20 minutes.

Note: Wheat germ, cracked wheat, and malt extract can be bought at the chemist or whole food store.

Starters

Choose the first course of every meal to set the scene. If you have little time to spare, freshly sliced tomatoes sprinkled with chopped parsley and onion take only a minute or two to prepare. Another time-saver—cook a few more French beans, courgettes, carrots, cauliflower florets or leeks than you need for the main meal and serve these cold as an hors d'oeuvre later, just tossed in French dressing.

Cream of chestnut soup

Imperial/Metric
1 lb./450 g. chestnuts
1 small onion
2 sticks celery
1 oz./25 g. butter
1 tablespoon plain flour
$\frac{3}{4}$ pint/4 dl. milk
$\frac{1}{2}$ pint/3 dl. water
salt and pepper
fried bread croûtons

American
1 lb. chestnuts
1 small onion
2 stalks celery
2 tablespoons butter
1 tablespoon all-purpose flour
2 cups milk
1$\frac{1}{4}$ cups water
salt and pepper
croûtons

Boil the chestnuts for 15-20 minutes. Shell and skin them. Cook in enough water to cover for 30 minutes, until they are tender. Strain, then sieve or liquidise the cooked chestnuts in a blender. Chop the onion and celery finely. Sauté in the butter until soft. Stir in the flour and cook for 2-3 minutes. Slowly add the milk, water and chestnut purée. Simmer gently for 15 minutes. Season to taste with salt and pepper and serve with croûtons.

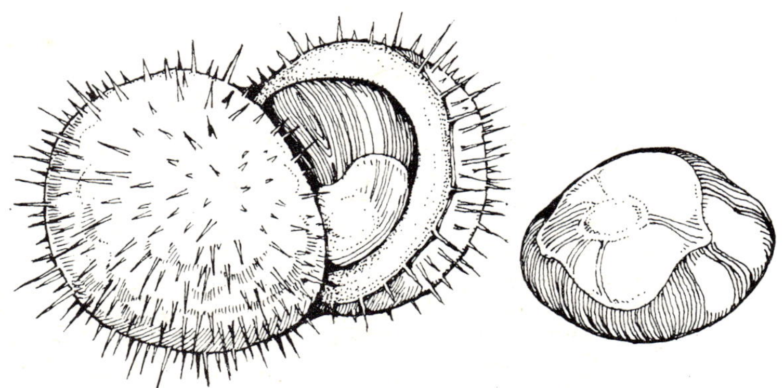

Hansel's curry soup

Imperial/Metric
1 oz./25 g. butter
1 small onion, chopped
1 tablespoon cornflour
1 teaspoon curry powder
8 oz./225 g. dessert apples, peeled and diced
1 pint/generous $\frac{1}{2}$ litre chicken stock
1 tablespoon lemon juice
$\frac{1}{4}$ pint/1$\frac{1}{2}$ dl. single cream
1 red skinned dessert apple
sprig of watercress

American
2 tablespoons butter
1 small onion, chopped
1 tablespoon cornstarch
1 teaspoon curry powder
2 medium eating apples, pared and diced
2$\frac{1}{2}$ cups chicken broth
1 tablespoon lemon juice
$\frac{1}{2}$ cup coffee cream
1 red skinned eating apple
sprig of watercress

Melt the butter in a saucepan. Fry the onion in the melted butter until limp, but not brown. Stir in the cornflour and curry powder. Cook for 2-3 minutes. Add the diced apples, chicken stock and lemon juice. Cover and simmer for 30 minutes. Liquidise in a blender or sieve. Pour into a clean saucepan. Stir in the single cream and reheat gently. Core and chop the apple, and cut a few watercress leaves into strips. Serve the soup with the chopped apple and watercress garnish.

Golden pumpkin soup

Imperial/Metric
2 lb./1 kg. pumpkin
1 small onion, finely
 chopped
2 tablespoons chopped
 green pepper
1 oz. /25 g. butter or
 margarine
½ pint/3 dl. milk
½ pint/3 dl. chicken stock
1 teaspoon salt
¼ teaspoon pepper
1 tablespoon tomato purée
few drops Worcestershire
 sauce
chopped chives

American
2 lb. pumpkin
1 small onion, finely
 chopped
2 tablespoons chopped
 green pepper
2 tablespoons butter or
 margarine
1¼ cups milk
1¼ cups chicken broth
1 teaspoon salt
¼ teaspoon pepper
1 tablespoon tomato paste
few drops Worcestershire
 sauce
chopped chives

Peel and remove seeds from the pumpkin. Steam until tender: then mash or liquidise until smooth. Sauté the onion and green pepper in the butter until soft. Stir in the pumpkin purée and milk, stock, salt, pepper, tomato purée and Worcestershire sauce. Serve very hot, garnished with chopped chives.

18

Courgette soup

Imperial/Metric
1 clove garlic
1 onion
2 lb./1 kg. courgettes
1 tablespoon olive oil
3 pints/1½ litres beef
  stock
½ teaspoon dried thyme
½ teaspoon dried sage
3 oz./75 g. long grain rice
pepper
4 tablespoons grated
  Parmesan cheese

American
1 clove garlic
1 onion
2 lb. zucchini
1 tablespoon olive oil
7½ cups beef broth
½ teaspoon dried thyme
½ teaspoon dried sage
½ cup long grain rice
pepper
4 tablespoons grated
  Parmesan cheese

Crush the garlic, chop the onion and slice the courgettes. Heat the oil in a saucepan and use to fry the garlic and onion until soft. Add the stock, bring to the boil and add the courgettes, thyme and sage. Sprinkle in the rice. Stir carefully and simmer for 15-20 minutes. Season the soup with the pepper and serve with grated Parmesan cheese sprinkled on top.

Avocado pears with fire'n ice tomatoes

Imperial/Metric
4 tomatoes
1 onion
4 ice cubes
4 fl oz./125 ml. white
  vinegar
1 teaspoon celery seed
½ teaspoon salt
¼ teaspoon dry mustard
pinch cayenne pepper
¼ teaspoon freshly ground
  black pepper
1 tablespoon castor sugar
2 avocado pears

American
4 tomatoes
1 onion
4 ice cubes
½ cup white vinegar
1 teaspoon celery seed
½ teaspoon salt
¼ teaspoon dry mustard
pinch cayenne pepper
¼ teaspoon freshly ground
  black pepper
1 tablespoon granulated
  sugar
2 avocado pears

Peel and slice the tomatoes and slice the onion. Place these in alternate layers in a deep bowl and add the ice cubes. Combine the vinegar, seasonings and sugar in a small saucepan and boil for 1 minute. Pour over the tomatoes and onion and chill until serving time. Peel and dice the avocado pears. Divide among 4 serving dishes. Drain the tomato and onion mixture and spoon over the avocado.

Pâté of pork with walnuts

Imperial/Metric
6 oz./175 g. streaky bacon
1½ lb./¾ kg. lean pork
8 oz./225 g. belly of pork
8 oz./225 g. walnuts
1 small onion
2 eggs
2 oz./50 g. fresh brown
  breadcrumbs
¼ teaspoon ground mace
½ teaspoon black pepper
1 teaspoon salt
2 tablespoons brandy
8 walnut halves
3 oz./75 g. butter, melted

American
6 slices side bacon
1½ lb. lean pork
8 oz. fresh picnic shoulder
2 cups walnuts
1 small onion
2 eggs
1 cup fresh brown
  bread crumbs
¼ teaspoon ground mace
½ teaspoon black pepper
1 teaspoon salt
2 tablespoons brandy
8 walnut halves
⅓ cup melted butter

Oil an earthenware dish or a 2 pint/
generous 1 litre casserole. Line with
the bacon rashers with the rinds removed.
Mince the meat with the walnuts and
onion until very fine. Beat the eggs lightly
and add to the meat mixture along with
the breadcrumbs, seasonings and brandy.
Press into the prepared dish, cover with
greaseproof paper or foil: put on the lid
and stand the dish in a bain marie, or a
roasting tin half filled with hot water.
Bake in a moderate oven (350°F, 180°C,
Gas Mark 4) for 3 hours. Remove the lid
and place a light weight on top. Leave
until cold. Remove paper and arrange the
walnut halves on top. Pour over the
melted butter. Store in the refrigerator.

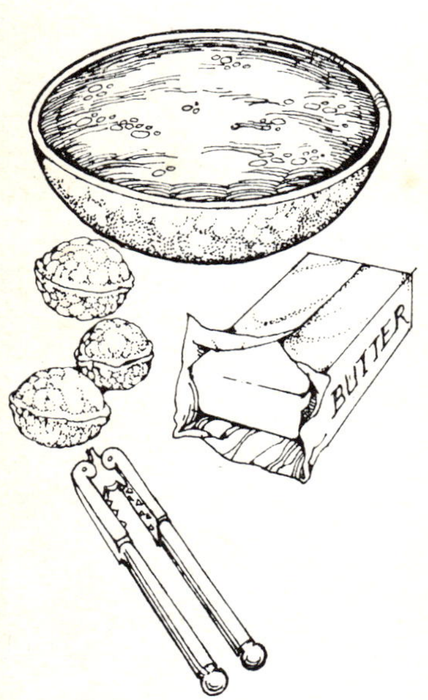

Canterbury cocktail

Imperial/Metric
1 large orange
juice of 1 lemon
6 fl.oz./175 ml. corn oil
2 teaspoons sugar
1 tablespoon chopped mint
  or tarragon
salt and pepper
3 ripe tomatoes
2 ripe Conference pears
4 red dessert apples
1 tablespoon lemon juice
sprigs of mint

American
1 large orange
juice of 1 lemon
¾ cup salad oil
2 teaspoons sugar
1 tablespoon chopped mint
  or tarragon
salt and pepper
3 ripe tomatoes
2 ripe firm pears
4 red eating apples
1 tablespoon lemon juice
sprigs of mint

Grate the zest from the orange and extract
the juice. Mix the orange juice with the
lemon juice, oil, sugar, chopped herbs
and seasoning. Pour into a deep bowl.
Skin the tomatoes and sieve the pulp into
the orange dressing, discarding the seeds.
Chop the flesh and add to the dressing.
Peel, core and chop the pears and three
of the apples. Add to the orange dressing.
Chill. To serve, spoon into 4 dishes.
Slice the remaining apple and dip in the
lemon juice. Arrange over each cocktail
and sprinkle with the grated orange zest
and sprigs of fresh mint.

Eggs in tomato concasse

Imperial/Metric	American
4 eggs	4 eggs
1 oz./25 g. butter	2 tablespoons butter
1 teaspoon oil	1 teaspoon oil
1 clove garlic	1 clove garlic
1 medium onion, chopped	1 medium onion, chopped
4 medium tomatoes	4 medium tomatoes
1 tablespoon tomato purée	1 tablespoon tomato paste
1 teaspoon sugar	1 teaspoon sugar
1 teaspoon dried thyme	1 teaspoon dried thyme
2 bay leaves	2 bay leaves
salt and pepper	salt and pepper
1½ oz./40 g. Gruyère cheese, grated	⅓ cup grated Gruyère cheese

Hard-boil the eggs and shell them. Meanwhile heat the butter and oil and use to cook the crushed garlic and chopped onion gently until soft. Chop the tomatoes and add to the pan with the tomato purée, sugar, herbs, bay leaves and seasoning to taste. Simmer gently, covered, until very thick, but do not allow to burn. Pass through a sieve. Divide the mixture between four ramekin dishes, gently lower the eggs into the ramekins, sprinkle with cheese and place under a hot grill until the cheese begins to melt.

 Apple and avocado salad

Imperial/Metric
2 avocado pears
2 dessert apples
1 bunch watercress
2 oz./50 g. salted
  peanuts
lemon dressing:
6 tablespoons olive oil
2 tablespoons lemon juice
salt and pepper
1 teaspoon mild Continental
  mustard
1 clove garlic, crushed
1 teaspoon castor sugar

American
2 avocado pears
2 dessert apples
1 bunch watercress
½ cup salted peanuts
lemon dressing:
½ cup olive oil
3 tablespoons lemon juice
salt and pepper
1 teaspoon mild mustard
1 clove garlic, crushed
1 teaspoon granulated
  sugar

Cut the avocados in half, discard the stones and remove the flesh without damaging the skins. Chop the flesh roughly. Core the apples and chop roughly. Reserve 4 sprigs of watercress for the garnish and chop the remainder. Chop the peanuts. Mix together all ingredients for the dressing and beat really well. Lightly toss the chopped avocado, apple, watercress and nuts in the dressing and pile back into the avocado shells. Garnish with watercress.

Spanish herrings

Imperial/Metric
4 fresh herrings
1 carrot
1 onion
1 small root horseradish
8 stuffed green olives,
  sliced
2 oz./50 g. castor sugar
4 tablespoons water
7 fl.oz./200 ml. white
  wine vinegar
2 teaspoons whole pickling
  spice
2 bay leaves

American
4 fresh herrings
1 carrot
1 onion
1 small root horseradish
8 sliced stuffed green
  olives
¼ cup granulated sugar
4 tablespoons water
⅞ cup white wine vinegar
2 teaspoons whole pickling
  spice
2 bay leaves

Have the herrings cleaned, boned and filleted. Thinly slice the carrot and onion, scrub and shred the horseradish and slice the olives. Put the sugar, water and vinegar in a pan, heat gently until sugar dissolves, then boil for 2 minutes. Cool. Plunge the herring fillets in boiling water for about 3 seconds, drain and scrape off the skins with a knife. Layer the herrings in a shallow 2 pint/generous 1 litre dish with the remaining ingredients. Pour the vinegar over, cover and chill for 2-3 days, turning occasionally.

Pears with Liptauer cheese

Imperial/Metric
3 oz./75 g. Demi-sel cheese
1 tablespoon single cream
1 teaspoon capers
1 teaspoon paprika pepper
salt and pepper
2 large eating pears
2 tablespoons Italian
    dressing
few lettuce leaves
$\frac{1}{2}$ cucumber, sliced
2 stuffed green olives,
    halved

American
3 oz. cream cheese
1 tablespoon coffee cream
1 teaspoon capers
1 teaspoon paprika pepper
salt and pepper
2 large eating pears
2 tablespoons Italian
    dressing
few lettuce leaves
$\frac{1}{2}$ cucumber, sliced
2 stuffed green olives,
    halved

First make the filling. Mash the cheese and cream with a fork, beat in the finely chopped capers, paprika and seasoning to taste. Peel, halve and core the pears and brush with the salad dressing to prevent discoloration. Arrange the pear halves, cut side uppermost, on individual plates on a bed of lettuce leaves and cucumber slices. Pipe or spoon the cheese mixture into the hollows and garnish each one with half a stuffed green olive.

Main dishes

Fish is plentiful, and trying out original ideas to present it is a pleasant adventure. Beef is at its best and pork traditionally comes in at Michaelmas. Here are some delicious ways to exploit both these favourite meats. Also, be prepared to welcome the opening of the game season with more than a brace of new recipes for birds and beasts.

Mackerel with apple stuffing

Imperial/Metric
2 medium mackerel
1 small onion
2 Bramley apples
4 oz./125 g. butter
3 oz./75 g. bread cubes
grated zest of $\frac{1}{2}$ lemon
1 tablespoon chopped
  parsley
pinch dried basil
salt and pepper
parsley sprigs

American
2 medium mackerel
1 small onion
2 tart apples
$\frac{1}{2}$ cup butter
1 cup bread cubes
grated rind of $\frac{1}{2}$ lemon
1 tablespoon chopped
  parsley
pinch basil
salt and pepper
parsley sprigs

Clean the mackerel and remove the heads. Chop the onion and one of the apples. Fry the chopped onion and apple in half of the butter until soft. Add the bread cubes, lemon zest, herbs and seasoning. Use to stuff the mackerel and secure with skewers. Bake in a moderate oven (350°F, 180°C, Gas Mark 4) for 40 minutes or until golden brown and cooked through. Core and slice the remaining apple and fry in the remaining butter until golden, turning once. Overlap the apple slices along each side of the mackerel and garnish with the parsley sprigs. Serves 2.

# Cassolettes of fish

Imperial/Metric
6 fl. oz./175 ml. dry white wine
1 sprig parsley
1 small onion
1 bay leaf
salt and pepper
4 oz./125 g. cod fillet
4 scallops
1 pint/generous $\frac{1}{2}$ litre
  mussels
1 oz./25 g. butter
2 tablespoons grated onion
$\frac{3}{4}$ oz./20 g. flour
1 egg yolk
4 tablespoons single cream

American
$\frac{3}{4}$ cup dry white wine
1 sprig parsley
1 small onion
1 bay leaf
salt and pepper
4 oz. cod fillet
4 scallops
$2\frac{1}{2}$ cups mussels
2 tablespoons butter
2 tablespoons grated onion
3 tablespoons all-purpose
  flour
1 egg yolk
4 tablespoons coffee cream

Make a court bouillon with the wine, $\frac{1}{4}$ pint/$1\frac{1}{2}$ dl. water, the parsley sprig, onion, bay leaf and seasoning. Poach the fish and scallops in this until just tender. Scrub the mussels, remove the 'beards', and bring to the boil in very little salted water so that they open. Discard any which do not open, remove the cooked mussels from the shells. Remove the fish and scallops from the poaching liquid, chop roughly, mix with the mussels and divide between four individual casseroles. Add the water from cooking the mussels to the court bouillon and strain carefully to make a measured $\frac{1}{2}$ pint/3 dl. Make up with extra wine if necessary. Melt the butter and stir in the grated onion. Cook until onion is transparent, then sprinkle in the flour and cook, stirring, for 1 minute. Gradually add the fish stock and bring to the boil, stirring constantly, until smooth and thickened. Lightly beat the egg yolk, whisk into the sauce, remove from the heat and stir in the cream. Taste and adjust seasoning, pour sauce over the casseroles. Place under a hot grill for a few minutes until brown on top and serve hot.

Smoked fish cream

Imperial/Metric
½ pint/3 dl. milk
12 oz./350 g. thick smoked
 cod fillet
1 oz./25 g. butter
¾ oz./20 g. flour
1 egg, separated
½ teaspoon French mustard
white pepper
4 tablespoons double cream
12 stuffed olives
½ pint/3 dl. liquid aspic
 jelly

American
1¼ cups milk
¾ lb. thick smoked cod
 fillet
2 tablespoons butter
4 tablespoons all purpose
 flour
1 egg, separated
½ teaspoon French mustard
white pepper
5 tablespoons heavy cream
12 stuffed olives
1½ cups liquid aspic

Place the milk in a saucepan and use to poach the cod fillet very gently for about 15 minutes, until tender. If necessary add 2 or 3 tablespoons of water. Remove fish from liquid and flake, discarding skin and bones. Strain the liquid from cooking the fish and make up to 6 fl. oz./2 dl./¾ cup if necessary with more milk. Melt the butter in a clean saucepan, stir in the flour and cook for 1 minute. Gradually add the measured liquid and bring to the boil, stirring constantly, until sauce is thick and smooth. Continue cooking for 2 minutes then beat in the egg yolk and remove from the heat. Taste and add mustard and white pepper. Pound up the fish and gradually add the sauce, or liquidise fish and sauce together in a blender. Place the mixture in a basin and stir in the cream. Beat the egg white until stiff, carefully fold into the mixture and use to fill a pie dish two-thirds full. Slice each stuffed olive into 4 and arrange the slices over the fish cream to cover as far as possible the surface of the mixture. Make up the aspic and chill until syrupy. Spoon over the cream and leave to set.

Fennel stuffed trout

Imperial/Metric
1 small onion
4 oz./125 g. mushrooms
2 oz./50 g. cooked long
 grain rice
1 head fennel, chopped
2 oz./50 g. butter, melted
salt and pepper
4 medium trout, cleaned
4 lemon wedges and
 fresh fennel leaves to
 garnish

American
1 small onion
1 cup mushrooms
½ cup cooked rice
1 head fennel, chopped
¼ cup melted butter
salt and pepper
4 medium trout, cleaned
4 lemon wedges and
 fresh fennel leaves to
 garnish

Chop the onion and mushrooms finely and mix with the rice, 2 tablespoons of the chopped fennel and the melted butter. Season with salt and pepper. Stuff the trout with the rice mixture. Wrap each trout in buttered foil and place in a baking tray. Bake in a moderately hot oven (375°F, 190°C, Gas Mark 5) for 25-30 minutes. Meanwhile cook the remaining fennel in boiling salted water until tender. Drain and place on a hot serving dish. Unwrap the trout, arrange on the fennel and garnish with the lemon wedges and fresh fennel leaves.

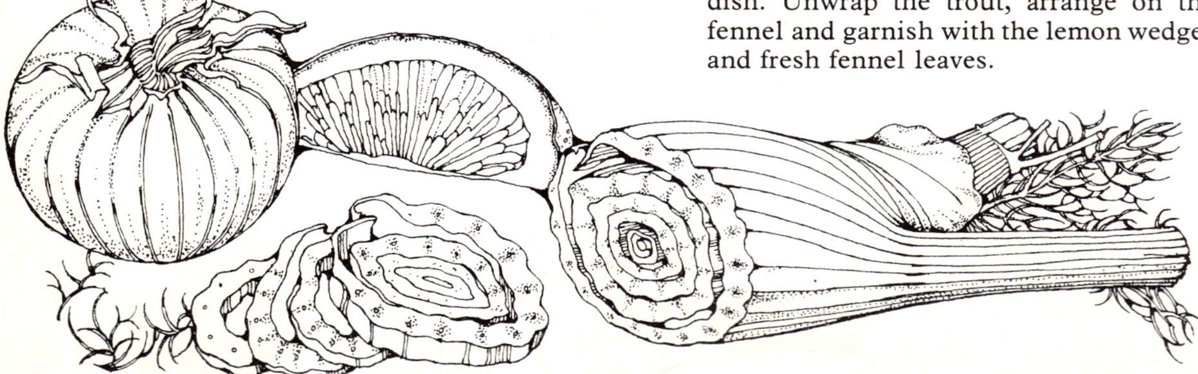

Sole with spiced butter

Imperial/Metric
4 oz./100 g. butter,
  clarified
1 tablespoon oil
salt and pepper
8 oz./225 g. fillets of sole
5 teaspoons lemon juice
1 oz./25 g. parsley,
  chopped
2 spring onions, chopped
1 teaspoon herb and spice
  blend for fish
lemon wedges
parsley sprigs

American
$\frac{1}{2}$ cup clarified butter
1 tablespoon oil
salt and pepper
$\frac{1}{2}$ lb. fillets of sole
5 teaspoons lemon juice
2 tablespoons chopped
  parsley
2 green onions, chopped
1 teaspoon herb and spice
  blend for fish
lemon wedges
parsley sprigs

Melt butter and oil together in a wide heavy frying pan. Season the fillets if required and sauté them over a high heat for 2-3 minutes on each side until golden brown. Transfer to a serving dish, sprinkle with lemon juice and keep hot. Add parsley, spring onion and spices to the pan and cook until butter turns brown but not burnt. Pour over fish and serve garnished with lemon wedges and parsley sprigs.

Haddock with tomato topping

Imperial/Metric
1 lb./450 g. onions
3 tablespoons oil
8 oz./225 g. mushrooms
salt and pepper
1 teaspoon dried thyme
1 teaspoon dried savory
1½ lb./¾ kg. fillet fresh
    haddock
6 small tomatoes
2 fl. oz./50 ml. white wine
2 oz./50 g. Gruyère cheese,
    grated

American
1 lb. onions
3 tablespoons oil
8 oz. mushrooms
salt and pepper
1 teaspoon dried thyme
1 teaspoon dried savory
1½ lb. fresh haddock
    fillets
6 small tomatoes
¼ cup white wine
½ cup grated Gruyère cheese

Cut the onions in very fine slices. Sauté in the oil until golden brown. When the onion is soft, add the sliced mushrooms and seasoning. Stir gently until the mushrooms begin to render their juice. Turn half the contents of the pan into a buttered ovenproof dish, sprinkle with some of the herbs. Arrange the fish on top, season and cover with the remaining onion mixture then with the quartered tomatoes. Pour over the wine, sprinkle with the rest of the herbs and the grated cheese. Place in a moderate oven (350°F., 180°C, Gas Mark 4) for 35 minutes.

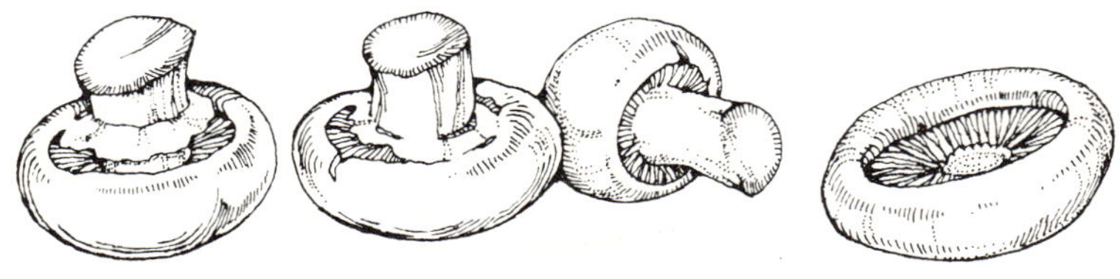

Fried cod with beetroot and horseradish cream

Imperial/Metric
8 small cod fillets
oil for frying
batter:
8 oz./225 g. self-raising
  flour
pinch salt
1 tablespoon oil
warm water
1 egg white
sauce:
1 small canned red
  pimiento
2 tablespoons finely
  diced apple
2 tablespoons finely
  diced beetroot
2 tablespoons grated
  horseradish
whipped double cream
salt and pepper
1 lemon and 1 bunch
  parsley to garnish

American
8 small cod fillets
oil for frying
batter:
2 cups all-purpose flour
2 teaspoons baking powder
pinch salt
1 tablespoon oil
warm water
1 egg white
sauce:
1 small canned red
  pimiento
2 tablespoons finely
  diced apple
2 tablespoons finely
  diced beets
2 tablespoons grated
  horseradish
whipped cream
salt and pepper
1 lemon and 1 bunch
  parsley to garnish

First make the batter. Put the flour and salt in a basin, make a well in the centre, pour in the oil and beat well, gradually drawing in the dry ingredients and adding sufficient warm water to give a smooth but fairly thick batter. Beat the egg white until stiff and fold into the batter. It improves if allowed to stand for a short while before using. To make the sauce, chop the pimiento very finely, fold in the apple, beetroot and horseradish and add sufficient cream to coat well. Season to taste and pile into a sauce boat. (A milder sauce can be made by decreasing the amount of horseradish and increasing the amount of beetroot and apple.) To cook the fish, dip the fillets into the batter and plunge straight into hot deep oil in a frying basket. Cook for 8-10 minutes, or until golden brown. Drain on absorbent kitchen paper and pile up on a warm serving dish. Garnish with knotted lemon halves and sprigs of parsley.

Knotted lemon halves: Cut the lemon in half and cut a tiny slice of rind from each end so the cut halves will sit firmly. Peel a sliver of rind about $\frac{1}{4}$ inch/$\frac{1}{2}$ cm. deep round each half, leaving about $\frac{1}{2}$ inch/ 1 cm. attached. Tie the long end into a single knot.

Scallops in cream

Imperial/Metric
6 scallops
4 peppercorns
1 teaspoon lemon juice
1 bay leaf
2 oz./50 g. butter
1 oz./25 g. plain flour
8 fl. oz./225 ml. single cream
salt and pepper
2 oz./50 g. sliced mushrooms
bread cases:
1 unsliced white sandwich loaf
1 egg, beaten
3 fl. oz./75 ml. milk
oil for frying

American
6 scallops
4 peppercorns
1 teaspoon lemon juice
1 bay leaf
¼ cup butter
¼ cup all-purpose flour
1 cup coffee cream
salt and pepper
½ cup sliced mushrooms
bread cases:
1 unsliced white bread loaf
1 egg, beaten
⅓ cup milk
oil for frying

First make the bread cases. Cut out 4 box shapes from the white loaf and scoop out the centres. Dip the bread cases in the beaten egg and milk and deep fry in hot oil until golden brown. Drain well and keep hot. Cover the scallops with cold water and add the peppercorns, lemon juice and bay leaf. Bring to the boil, reduce the heat and poach for 5 minutes. Drain and dice the scallops. Remove the bay leaf. Boil the cooking liquid to reduce it to ¼ pint/1½ dl. Melt half the butter in a saucepan, add the diced scallops and cook gently for 5 minutes. Stir in the flour and cook 2-3 minutes. Gradually add the cooking liquid. Cook until thick, then gradually stir in the cream. Season to taste. Spoon into the hot bread cases. Fry the mushrooms in the remaining butter and scatter over the scallop mixture.

Whittington's whitebait

Imperial/Metric
1 oz./25 g. flour
½ teaspoon paprika pepper
pinch cayenne pepper
salt
1 lb./450 g. whitebait
oil for frying

American
¼ cup all-purpose flour
½ teaspoon paprika pepper
pinch cayenne pepper
salt
1 lb. whitebait
oil for frying

Season the flour with the paprika, cayenne and salt and use to coat the whitebait twice. Cook the whitebait in a frying basket in deep hot oil for about 2 minutes until almost cooked, drain and reheat the oil until really hot. Plunge the fish in the oil again until golden brown. Drain well, serve with lemon wedges and brown bread and butter.

Party pasta with mussels

Imperial/Metric
4 pints/2½ litres fresh
   mussels
8 fl. oz./225 ml. dry white
   wine
2 tablespoons chopped
   parsley
1 tablespoon chopped
   shallots or onion
8 oz./225 g. pasta shells
2 oz./50 g. butter
grated zest of ½ lemon
¼ teaspoon freshly ground
   black pepper
8 oz./227 g. tomatoes,
   chopped
salt and pepper
2 fl. oz./50 ml. single cream
lemon juice

American
2¾ quarts fresh mussels
1 cup dry white wine
2 tablespoons chopped
   parsley
1 tablespoon chopped
   shallots or onion
2½ cups pasta shells
¼ cup butter
grated rind of ½ lemon
¼ teaspoon freshly ground
   black pepper
1 cup chopped tomatoes
salt and pepper
¼ cup coffee cream
lemon juice

Scrub the mussel shells and scrape off the 'beards'. Place in a large saucepan with the wine, one tablespoon of the chopped parsley and the shallots. Cover and simmer over low heat until they open, about 15 minutes. Discard any which remain closed. Remove the mussels and pull the top shells off. Meanwhile, cook the pasta shells in boiling salted water for 8-10 minutes or until just tender. Drain and toss with the butter, lemon zest and black pepper. Turn into a serving dish and arrange the mussels in the half shells over the pasta. Cover and keep hot. Add the tomatoes to the wine liquid. Season with salt and pepper. Boil for 5 minutes. Remove from the heat and stir in the cream. Add lemon juice to taste. Pour the sauce over the mussels and pasta. Garnish with the remaining chopped parsley.

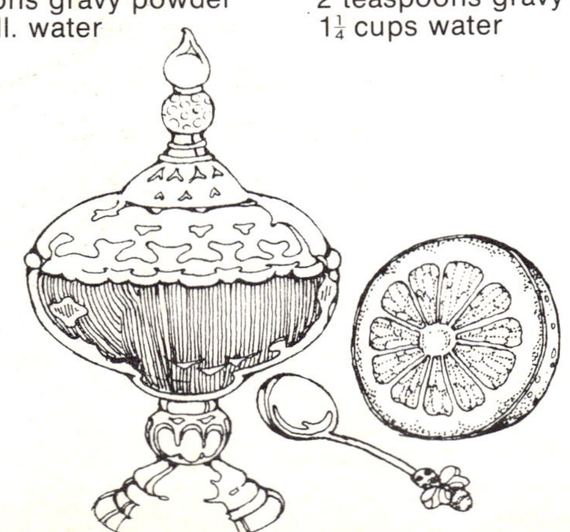

★ Honey and orange pork roast

Imperial/Metric
2½-3 lb./1¼-1½ kg. joint
  belly pork
salt
1 orange
1 tablespoon clear honey
2 teaspoons gravy powder
½ pint/3 dl. water

American
2½-3 lb. fresh picnic
  shoulder
salt
1 orange
1 tablespoon clear honey
2 teaspoons gravy powder
1¼ cups water

Score, roll and tie the joint into a neat shape. Sprinkle with salt. Roast in a moderate oven (350°F, 180°C, Gas Mark 4) for 35 minutes per pound/450 g. plus 35 minutes over. Finely grate the zest from the orange and squeeze the juice. Remove cooked joint on to a hot serving dish and keep warm. Skim surplus fat from the roasting tin, stir in the honey and orange zest and juice. Moisten the gravy powder with a little of the water, add the rest to the roasting tin and stir well. Bring the juices from the pan to the boil in a small saucepan, stir in the gravy mix and cook, stirring, over low heat until thick and smooth. If a crisp crackling is not required, brush the skin of the joint with a little extra clear honey 30 minutes before the end of cooking time. Serves 6.

Perfection pork with celery

Imperial/Metric
1 lb. 8 oz./¾ kg. pork
   fillet
1½ oz./40 g. butter
8 oz./225 g. carrots
4 sticks celery
1 teaspoon salt
freshly ground black pepper
1 teaspoon cumin powder
¾ pint/4 dl. chicken stock
1 teaspoon cornflour

American
1 lb. 8 oz. pork tenderloin
3 tablespoons butter
3 medium carrots
4 stalks celery
1 teaspoon salt
freshly ground black pepper
1 teaspoon cumin powder
2 cups chicken broth
1 teaspoon cornstarch

Cut the pork into very thin slices. Sauté in the butter for two minutes. Slice the carrots into julienne strips. Slice the celery sticks diagonally. Add the carrots, celery, seasonings and chicken stock to the pork. Simmer for six minutes or until the vegetables are just tender. Remove the meat and vegetables to a hot serving dish. Mix the cornflour with a little cold water and pour into the hot stock. Simmer until the sauce thickens and clears, stirring constantly. Taste and adjust seasonings. Pour the sauce over the meat and vegetables. Serve with noodles, and a very hotly spiced fruit chutney.

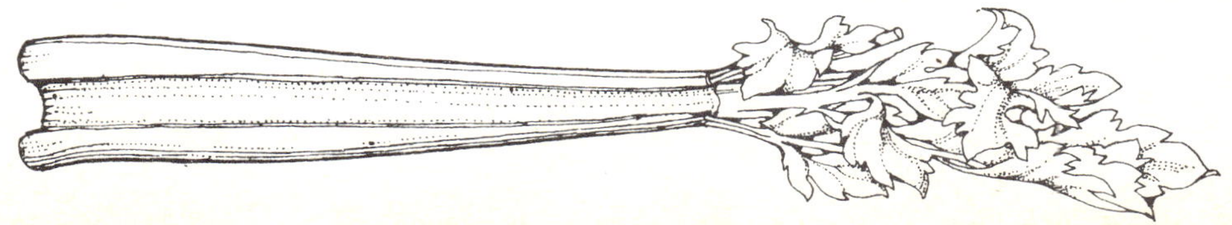

Tourte au chou

Imperial/Metric
10 oz./275 g. shortcrust
 pastry
1 small green cabbage
12 oz./350 g. cooked meat
2 oz./50 g. streaky bacon
1 large onion
sprig parsley
2 oz./50 g. butter
½ teaspoon dried thyme
pinch ground allspice
salt and pepper
1 egg

American
10 oz. basic pie dough
1 small green cabbage
12 oz. cooked meat
2 slices side bacon
1 large onion
sprig parsley
¼ cup butter
½ teaspoon dried thyme
pinch ground allspice
salt and pepper
1 egg

Roll out two-thirds of the pastry to line a deep 8 inch/20 cm. flan tin. Chop the cabbage finely and blanch in fast boiling salted water for 8 minutes. Drain well. Meanwhile, mince together the meat, bacon, onion and parsley. Melt the butter, turn the meat mixture in this, adding the herbs, spices and seasoning to taste, until well blended and lightly browned. Place half the cabbage in the flan case, cover with the meat mixture and put the remaining cabbage on top. Roll out rest of pastry to make a lid, slightly larger than the flan case. Use lid to cover the tourte, dampen the edges and fold down over the pastry base inside the edge of the flan tin. Cut a steam vent in the centre and surround with a circle made from pastry trimmings. Brush the pastry well with beaten egg. Bake in a moderate oven (375°F, 190°C, Gas Mark 5) for 30 minutes. Remove tourte from oven, brush with remaining egg and return to the oven for a further 10 minutes. When golden brown, remove from oven and serve hot.

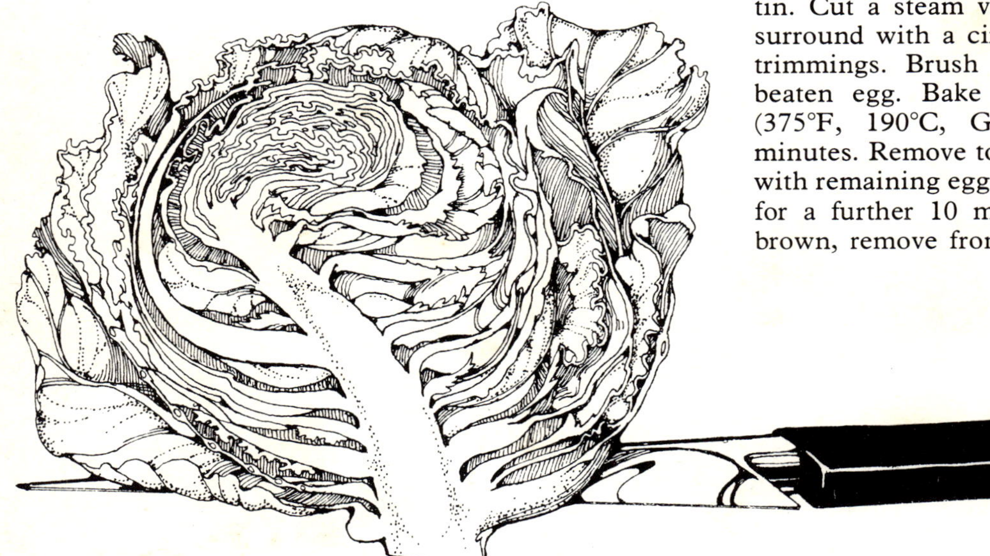

Lamb's liver Magyar style

Imperial/Metric
1 large onion
4 oz./125 g. mushrooms
2 oz./50 g. butter
1 lb./450 g. lamb's liver
2 tablespoons plain flour
salt and pepper
pinch nutmeg
pinch mace
¼ pint/1½ dl. dry white
 wine
¼ pint/1½ dl. soured cream
watercress

American
1 large onion
4 oz. mushrooms
¼ cup butter
1 lb. lamb's liver
2 tablespoons all-purpose
 flour
salt and pepper
pinch nutmeg
pinch mace
½ cup dry white wine
½ cup soured cream
watercress

Slice the onion and mushrooms and sauté in half of the butter until soft. Lift out and keep warm. Slice the liver into narrow strips. Season the flour with the salt and pepper. Toss the liver strips in the seasoned flour and fry in the remaining butter until browned. Add the nutmeg, mace, and white wine. Bring to the boil and stir in the onions and mushrooms. Add the soured cream, reheat gently without boiling. Serve with hot sauté potatoes and garnish with watercress.

FARINE

Lambs' kidney sauté

Imperial/Metric
1 lb./450 g. lambs' kidneys
1 orange
1 oz./25 g. butter
2 tablespoons oil
2 large onions, sliced
4 tablespoons dry sherry
1 tablespoon Worcester-
  shire sauce
$\frac{1}{4}$ pint/1$\frac{1}{2}$ dl. beef stock
4 oz./100 g. button
  mushrooms, halved
1 tablespoon cornflour
salt and pepper

American
1 lb. lamb kidneys
1 orange
2 tablespoons butter
3 tablespoons oil
2 large onions, sliced
5 tablespoons dry sherry
1 tablespoon Worcester-
  shire sauce
$\frac{2}{3}$ cup beef stock
1 cup halved button
  mushrooms
1 tablespoon cornstarch
salt and pepper

Skin the kidneys, cut in half and snip out the cores. Remove the zest from the orange and cut into thin strips. Squeeze the juice. Heat together the butter and oil in a frying pan and use to fry the onion gently until softened but not browned. Add the kidneys and cook lightly until they turn brown on both sides. Add the orange zest and juice to the pan with the sherry, Worcestershire sauce, and stock. Bring to boiling point, add the mushrooms, cover and cook gently for about 5 minutes. Moisten the cornflour with a little cold water, add to the pan and bring to the boil, stirring until sauce thickens. Cook for a further 2 minutes. Adjust seasoning. Serve with freshly boiled noodles.

# Braised beef with mustard

Imperial/Metric
2 teaspoons dry mustard
2 tablespoons vinegar
3 tablespoons tomato purée
2 tablespoons corn oil
1 small onion, chopped
2 tablespoons brown sugar
1 teaspoon dried mixed herbs
salt and pepper
½ oz./15 g. dripping
2½-3 lb./1¼-1½ kg. joint silverside or brisket
3 large onions, quartered
3 large carrots, quartered
2 teaspoons cornflour

American
2 teaspoons dry mustard
2 tablespoons vinegar
3 tablespoons tomato paste
2 tablespoons corn oil
1 small onion, chopped
2 tablespoons brown sugar
1 teaspoon dried mixed herbs
salt and pepper
1 tablespoon drippings
2½-3 lb. boneless beef brisket
3 large onions, quartered
3 large carrots, quartered
2 teaspoons cornstarch

Mix together the mustard and vinegar. Add the tomato purée, oil, onion, sugar, herbs and seasoning to taste and blend well together to make a sauce. Heat the dripping in a heavy saucepan and use to brown the joint all over. Add the onions and carrots round the joint and pour the sauce over the meat. Cover with a close-fitting lid and simmer gently for 2½-3 hours, until the meat is tender. Remove joint to a warm serving dish, surround with the vegetables and keep hot. Moisten the cornflour with a little cold water and use to thicken the pan juices. Cook for 2 minutes, stirring constantly, and strain over the meat. Serves 8, or one hot meal for 4 and one cold meal.

Fruited lamb curry

Imperial/Metric
1 lb. 4oz./575 g. boned
  leg or shoulder of lamb
2 tablespoons flour
salt and pepper
1 medium onion
1 tablespoon oil
1 tablespoon curry powder
2 teaspoons curry paste
¾ pint/4 dl. stock or water
1 apple
1 tablespoon sultanas
2 oz./50 g. dried apricots
2 tablespoons lemon juice

American
1 lb. 4 oz. boned
  leg or shoulder of lamb
2 tablespoons flour
salt and pepper
1 medium onion
1 tablespoon oil
1 tablespoon curry powder
2 teaspoons curry paste
2 cups stock or water
1 apple
1 tablespoon golden
  raisins
⅓ cup dried apricots
2 tablespoons lemon juice

Trim excess fat from lamb and dice. Turn in flour seasoned with the salt and pepper. Chop the onion. Fry the lamb and onion in the oil until well browned. Stir in the curry powder and curry paste and cook for 2-3 minutes. Gradually stir in the stock or water. Bring to the boil and simmer for 10 minutes. Peel and chop the apple and add to the meat. Stir in the sultanas, apricots and lemon juice. Cover and simmer for one hour or until the meat is tender. Serve with plain boiled rice and a variety of accompaniments: onion rings, sliced tomatoes, desiccated coconut, peanuts, sliced bananas and poppadoms.

Sweetbreads in lemon butter sauce

Imperial/Metric
1 lb./450 g. sweetbreads
1 slice of lemon
2 oz./50 g. butter
2 tablespoons lemon juice
2 tablespoons chopped
  parsley
½ teaspoon salt
pinch pepper

American
1 lb. fresh or frozen
  sweetbreads
1 slice of lemon
¼ cup butter
2 tablespoons lemon juice
2 tablespoons chopped
  parsley
½ teaspoon salt
pinch pepper

Soak the sweetbreads in salted water with a few drops of vinegar added for several hours. Drain, cover with cold water and add a slice of lemon. Simmer for 20 minutes but do not boil. Drain, remove membranes and slice. Sauté in the butter for 5 minutes on each side. Stir in the lemon juice, parsley, salt and pepper. Heat through. Serve with hot cooked rice or buttered toast.

Green lasagne with beef

Imperial/Metric
8 oz./225 g. green lasagne
1 tablespoon oil
sauce:
1 large onion
1 large carrot
1 large green pepper
1 clove garlic
4 oz./100 g. streaky bacon
1 oz./25 g. butter
1 lb./450 g. minced beef
14 oz./400 g. can tomatoes
2 tablespoons tomato
  purée
½ teaspoon dried mixed
  herbs
¼ pint/1½ dl. beef stock
½ teaspoon sugar
salt and pepper

American
½ lb. green lasagne
1 tablespoon oil
sauce:
1 large onion
1 large carrot
1 large green sweet pepper
1 clove garlic
¼ lb. bacon slices
2 tablespoons butter
1 lb. ground beef
14 oz. can tomatoes
3 tablespoons tomato
  paste
½ teaspoon dried mixed
  herbs
⅔ cup beef stock
½ teaspoon sugar
salt and pepper

First make the sauce. Chop the onion and carrot, deseed and chop the green pepper, crush the garlic and derind and chop the bacon. Melt the butter and use to fry the onion, carrot, green pepper, garlic, bacon and minced beef until lightly browned. Add the tomatoes, tomato purée, herbs, stock, sugar and a little seasoning. Stir well, bring to the boil and cook for 30 minutes. Adjust the seasoning. Meanwhile break each strip of lasagne in half then cook in boiling salted water for about 10 minutes, until just tender. Drain well and toss lightly with the oil over low heat to separate. Keep hot. Arrange a bed of cooked lasagne in a shallow serving dish and pour the meat into the centre.

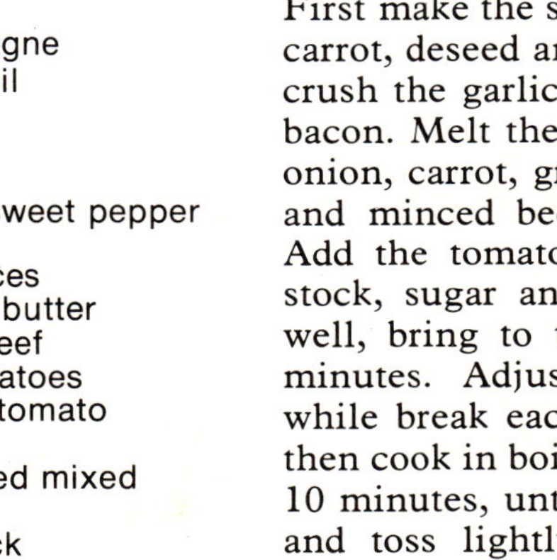

Californian beef crust pie

Imperial/Metric
1 egg
2 oz./50 g. soft
 breadcrumbs
3 fl. oz./1 dl. dry
 white wine
1 teaspoon onion salt
½ teaspoon celery salt
¼ teaspoon pepper
1 lb./450 g. minced beef
12 oz./330 g. grated potato
1 tablespoon grated onion
2 tablespoons chopped
 green pepper
1 tablespoon chopped
 canned red pimiento
¾ teaspoon salt
1 oz./25 g. butter
1½ oz./40 g. grated Cheddar
 cheese

American
1 egg
⅔ cup soft bread crumbs
⅓ cup dry white wine
1 teaspoon onion salt
½ teaspoon celery salt
¼ teaspoon pepper
1 lb. ground lean beef
12 oz. package frozen
 hash brown potatoes,
 defrosted
1 tablespoon instant
 minced onion
2 tablespoons chopped
 green pepper
1½ tablespoons chopped
 canned red pimiento
¾ teaspoon salt
2 tablespoons butter
⅓ cup grated Cheddar
 cheese

Beat the egg lightly and add the bread-crumbs, wine, onion and celery salts, and pepper and allow to stand for 1 minute to soak. Add the beef and mix until well blended. Pat the mixture into a greased shallow ovenproof dish to make a thick shell. Build up the sides slightly. Combine the potato with the onion, green pepper, pimiento and salt and spoon into the centre of the meat shell. Melt the butter and pour over the potatoes. Bake in a moderately hot oven (375°F, 190°C, Gas Mark 5) for 35 minutes. Sprinkle with cheese and bake for a further 5 minutes, until the cheese melts. Serve in wedges. *Note:* The Californian version uses the local Sauterne which is dry not sweet.

Chicken-courgette crêpes

Imperial/Metric
2 tablespoons chopped onion
2 tablespoons chopped celery
1 tablespoon butter
1 tablespoon plain flour
¼ pint/1½ dl. evaporated milk
4 oz./125 g. diced cooked chicken
few drops Worcestershire sauce
salt and pepper
2 medium courgettes
2 beaten eggs
1 oz./25 g. plain flour
2 tablespoons grated Parmesan cheese
1 teaspoon chopped chives
pinch salt and pepper
2 oz./50 g. grated cheese

American
2 tablespoons chopped onion
2 tablespoons chopped celery
1 tablespoon butter
1 tablespoon all-purpose flour
⅔ cup evaporated milk
1 cup diced cooked chicken
few drops Worcestershire sauce
salt and pepper
2 medium zucchini
2 beaten eggs
¼ cup all-purpose flour
2 tablespoons grated Parmesan cheese
1 teaspoon chopped chives
pinch salt and pepper
½ cup grated cheese

Sauté the onion and celery in the butter until limp. Stir in the flour and cook for 2 minutes. Gradually stir in the evaporated milk. Add the chicken, Worcestershire sauce, salt and pepper. Heat through. Keep warm while preparing the courgette crêpes. Peel and shred the courgettes. Mix with the eggs, flour, Parmesan cheese, chives and seasonings. Beat well. Lightly oil a small frying pan. Spoon a small amount of the courgette batter into the frying pan, spread evenly. Cook until browned, turn over and cook the other side. Continue to make the crêpes until the batter is finished. Spoon the prepared chicken filling on one side of each crêpe. Fold over and arrange in a lightly greased baking dish, sprinkle the crêpes with the grated cheese. Bake in a moderately hot oven (400°F, 200°C, Gas Mark 6) for 10 minutes.

Chicken with black olive sauce

Imperial/Metric
4 chicken portions
5 tablespoons oil
salt and pepper
1 lb./450 g. tomatoes
3 oz./75 g. black olives
1 large mild onion, chopped
2 chicken stock cubes
½ teaspoon dried oregano
1 teaspoon sugar
½ teaspoon celery salt
3 bay leaves
½ teaspoon paprika pepper
¼ pint/1½ dl. water
1 tablespoon cornflour

American
4 chicken portions
6 tablespoons oil
salt and pepper
1 lb. tomatoes
½ cup black olives
1 large mild onion, chopped
2 chicken bouillon cubes
½ teaspoon dried oregano
1 teaspoon sugar
½ teaspoon celery salt
3 bay leaves
½ teaspoon paprika pepper
generous ½ cup water
1 tablespoon cornstarch

Brush the chicken portions with some of the oil, sprinkle with salt and pepper and cook under a medium hot grill for 25-35 minutes, turning frequently. Meanwhile, peel the tomatoes and chop them if large. Stone and halve the olives. Cook the onion gently in the remaining oil until limp, stirring, for 2 minutes. Add the tomatoes, crumbled stock cubes, oregano, sugar, celery salt, bay leaves, paprika and water and bring to the boil, stirring constantly. Cover and cook gently for 20 minutes. Taste and adjust seasoning. Moisten the cornflour with 2 tablespoons cold water, stir into the sauce and cook, stirring constantly until the sauce thickens. Cook for a further 2 minutes. Serve the chicken with the sauce poured over.

Chicken with sesame seeds

Imperial/Metric
3 oz./75 g. plain flour
salt and pepper
1 tablespoon sesame seeds
½ teaspoon ground
  coriander
¼ teaspoon ground ginger
pinch chilli powder
4 chicken breasts
3 oz./75 g. butter
1 tablespoon olive oil
½ pint/3 dl. chicken stock
3 tablespoons dry white
  wine
1 tablespoon chopped
  parsley
1 tablespoon chopped
  watercress
2 sprigs fresh rosemary,
  stripped
¼ pint/1½ dl. double cream
6 oz./175 g. long grain
  rice
1 tablespoon melted butter

American
¾ cup all-purpose flour
salt and pepper
1 tablespoon sesame seeds
½ teaspoon ground
  coriander
¼ teaspoon ground ginger
dash chili powder
4 chicken breasts
⅓ cup butter
1 tablespoon olive oil
1¼ cups chicken broth
3 tablespoons dry white
  wine
1 tablespoon chopped parsley
1 tablespoon chopped
  watercress
2 sprigs fresh rosemary,
  stripped
½ cup whipping cream
1 cup long grain rice
1 tablespoon melted butter

Season the flour with the salt, pepper, sesame seeds, coriander, ginger and chilli powder. Coat the chicken portions evenly. Fry the chicken portions in the butter and olive oil for 10 minutes on each side. Transfer the chicken to a warm dish and keep hot. Stir the remaining seasoned flour into the frying pan; add the chicken stock, rosemary and wine. Bring to the boil, simmer gently for 20 minutes, or until reduced by half. Add remaining chopped herbs to sauce. Stir in the cream and reheat gently. Cook the rice in boiling salted water for 12 minutes. Drain and rinse with hot water. Stir in the melted butter. Pile the rice into a serving dish and arrange the chicken portions on top. Hand the sauce in a sauceboat.

Royal marmalade-glazed duck

Imperial/Metric
3 lb./1½ kg. roasting duck
1 teaspoon salt
8 oz./225 g. king-cut
   marmalade
¼ pint/1½ dl. dry sherry
½ pint/3 dl. chicken stock
1 teaspoon cornflour
salt and pepper.
parsley or watercress

American
3 lb. roasting duck
1 teaspoon salt
1 cup rough-cut
   marmalade
½ cup dry sherry
1¼ cups chicken broth
1 teaspoon cornstarch
salt and pepper
parsley or watercress

Prick the skin of the duck and sprinkle with the salt. Place the duck on a wire rack in a roasting pan and roast in a hot oven (425°F, 220°C, Gas Mark 7) for 30 minutes. Heat the marmalade and sherry until blended and brush one half of this mixture over the duck. Return the duck to a moderate oven (350°F, 180°C, Gas Mark 4) for one hour. Mix a little of the stock with the cornflour and bring the remaining stock to the boil. Stir the cornflour paste into the stock and cook until thickened, stirring constantly. Stir the remaining marmalade and sherry mixture into the sauce. Season to taste with salt and pepper. Garnish the duck with parsley or watercress and hand the sauce in a sauceboat.

Gingered autumn chicken

Imperial/Metric
6 chicken portions
flour for coating
2 tablespoons oil
1 large onion, chopped
1 chicken stock cube
3 pieces stem
  ginger, chopped
½ teaspoon ground ginger
2 bay leaves
3 medium Conference pears
2 medium Cox's Orange
  Pippins
8 oz./225 g. plums
2 tablespoons ginger syrup
lemon juice to taste
salt and pepper
1 tablespoon chopped
  parsley

American
6 chicken pieces
flour for coating
3 tablespoons oil
1 large onion, chopped
1 chicken bouillon cube
3 pieces stem ginger,
  chopped
½ teaspoon ground ginger
2 bay leaves
3 medium cooking pears
2 medium eating
  apples
½ lb. plums
3 tablespoons ginger syrup
lemon juice to taste
salt and pepper
1 tablespoon chopped
  parsley

Divide the chicken portions into serving-size pieces and coat with flour. Heat the oil in a flameproof casserole and use to fry the chicken pieces until crisp and golden brown all over. Remove chicken from the pan. Add the onion to the remaining fat and fry gently until just turning colour. Return the chicken pieces to the pan. Make up the stock cube with ¾ pint/4 dl./scant 2 cups boiling water and stir in the chopped ginger, and the ground ginger, and pour over the chicken. Bring to the boil, add bay leaves, cover and simmer gently for 20 minutes. Peel, core and slice the pears and apples. Halve and stone the plums. Add the fruit and ginger syrup to the casserole. Cover and simmer gently until the chicken is tender. Add lemon juice to taste and adjust seasoning. Serve garnished with chopped parsley. Serves 6.

Pigeon with orange sauce

Imperial/Metric
2 tablespoons oil
3 pigeons
1 onion
1 tablespoon redcurrant
  jelly
$\frac{1}{4}$ pint/$1\frac{1}{2}$ dl. chicken stock
$\frac{1}{4}$ pint/$1\frac{1}{2}$ dl. orange juice
salt and pepper
2 teaspoons cornflour
few orange slices and
  sprigs of watercress to
  garnish

American
3 tablespoons oil
3 pigeons
1 onion
1 tablespoon redcurrant
  jelly
$\frac{1}{2}$ cup chicken broth
$\frac{1}{2}$ cup orange juice
salt and pepper
2 teaspoons cornstarch
few orange slices and
  sprigs of watercress to
  garnish

Heat the oil in a frying pan and fry the pigeons until golden brown. Remove and put into a casserole. Finely chop the onion, add to the frying pan and cook gently until soft. Stir in the jelly, stock, orange juice and salt and pepper to taste. Stir well and pour over the pigeons. Cover casserole with a tight fitting lid and cook in a moderate oven (325°F, 170°C, Gas Mark 3) for 2 hours. Remove pigeons, place on a hot serving dish and keep warm. Strain the pan juices into a saucepan and stir in the cornflour moistened with 2 tablespoons cold water. Bring to the boil, stirring constantly, and cook until sauce is thickened and smooth. Garnish the pigeons with slices of fresh orange and watercress and hand the sauce separately. Serves 3.

Barbecued venison steaks

Imperial/Metric
3 lb./$1\frac{1}{2}$ kg. leg of venison
salt and pepper
cooking oil
8 fl. oz./225 ml. tomato
  juice
1 teaspoon salt
4 slices lemon
1 onion, sliced
2 tablespoons tomato purée
$\frac{1}{2}$ teaspoon chilli powder
$\frac{1}{4}$ teaspoon pepper

American
3 lb. venison leg
salt and pepper
cooking oil
1 cup tomato juice
1 teaspoon salt
4 slices lemon
1 onion, sliced
2 tablespoons tomato paste
$\frac{1}{2}$ teaspoon chili powder
$\frac{1}{4}$ teaspoon pepper

Slice the venison into 4 thick steaks. Season the steaks with salt and pepper. Brown in hot oil on both sides then place in a casserole dish. Combine the remaining ingredients and pour over the browned steaks. Bake in a moderate oven (325°F, 170°C, Gas Mark 3) for $1\frac{1}{2}$-2 hours. Baste with the sauce frequently during cooking.

Pheasant in brandy sauce

Imperial/Metric
1 young pheasant
1 small onion
pheasant liver
2 oz./50 g. streaky bacon
2 tablespoons oil
1 oz./25 g. butter
4 tablespoons brandy
4 oz./100g. mushrooms,
　sliced
½ pint/3 dl. red wine
¼ pint/1½ dl. double
　cream
salt and freshly ground black
　pepper watercress sprigs and
　fried bread triangles to
　garnish

American
1 young pheasant
1 small onion
pheasant liver
3 bacon slices
3 tablespoons oil
2 tablespoons butter
⅓ cup brandy
1 cup sliced mushrooms
1¼ cups red wine
⅔ cup heavy cream
salt and freshly ground black
　pepper watercress sprigs and
　fried bread triangles to
　garnish

Prepare the pheasant. Chop the onion finely and mix with the chopped pheasant liver. Put the mixture inside the pheasant. Remove the bacon rinds and chop the rashers finely. Place in a heavy, flameproof pan and heat until the fat runs. Increase the heat to brown the chopped bacon. Remove the bacon and keep aside. Add the oil and butter to the fat remaining in the pan, heat and brown the pheasant on all sides. Warm the brandy and pour it over the pheasant. Ignite and shake the pan backwards and forwards until the flames subside. Return the bacon to the pan, add the mushrooms, wine and seasoning. Cover tightly and simmer for 1 hour. Arrange the pheasant on a serving dish and keep hot. Place the flameproof casserole on the heat and whisk in the cream. Whisk over a moderate heat until the sauce is smooth. Check the seasoning, then pour over the pheasant and serve garnished with sprigs of watercress and triangles of fried bread. Serves 2-4.
Note: Triangles of bread may be prepared and fried in advance and stored in a polythene container in the freezer to serve with this and other game or poultry casseroles.

Cabbage-wrapped partridge

Imperial/Metric
2 partridges
salt and pepper
4 slices streaky bacon
8 oz./225 g. shredded
　cabbage
8 cabbage leaves
1 oz./25 g. butter
½ pint/3 dl. chicken stock
1 carrot, diced
1 tablespoon chopped
　onion
1 teaspoon salt
¼ teaspoon pepper
¼ teaspoon dried thyme
1 tablespoon cornflour

American
2 partridges
salt and pepper
4 slices side bacon
2 cups shredded cabbage
8 cabbage leaves
2 tablespoons butter
1¼ cups chicken broth
1 carrot, diced
1 tablespoon chopped
　onion
1 teaspoon salt
¼ teaspoon pepper
¼ teaspoon dried thyme
1 tablespoon cornstarch

Clean the partridges, removing any pinfeathers. Sprinkle the insides with salt and pepper. Fry the bacon until crisp; drain and dice. Mix the cooked diced bacon with the shredded cabbage. Stuff the partridges with the bacon-cabbage mixture. Wrap each partridge in 4 cabbage leaves. Tie with string. Place the cabbage-wrapped partridges in a large, deep pan and dot with the butter. Combine the chicken stock, carrot, onion and seasonings and pour over the partridges. Cover tightly and simmer for 45 minutes. Remove cabbage leaves and discard. Transfer the partridges to a hot serving dish and strain the cooking liquid. Mix the cornflour with a little cold water; add to the strained cooking liquid and cook until the sauce thickens. Serve the sauce with the partridges.

Baked hare with cranberries and chestnuts

Imperial/Metric
1 hare, jointed
3 oz./75 g. seasoned flour
2 tablespoons oil
2 oz./50g. butter
2 large onions, sliced
¾ pint/4 dl. beef stock
4 tablespoons Marsala
1 lb./450 g. chestnuts
8 oz./225 g. cranberries
salt and pepper

American
1 hare, jointed
¾ cup seasoned flour
3 tablespoons oil
¼ cup butter
2 large onions, sliced
scant 2 cups beef stock
5 tablespoons Marsala
1 lb. chestnuts
½ lb. cranberries
salt and pepper

Coat the hare joints and liver in the seasoned flour and brown all over in the hot oil and butter. Transfer joints to an ovenproof casserole, and add the sliced onion, stock and Marsala. Pour over the pan juices from browning the hare. Cover and cook in a moderate oven (325°F, 170°C, Gas Mark 3) for 2 hours. Meanwhile, boil the chestnuts for 15-20 minutes, or until the shell and skin can easily be removed. Add to the casserole with the cranberries, sprinkle in any remaining seasoned flour and stir gently. Cover and return to the oven for a further 20 minutes. Adjust seasoning.

Rabbit with game sauce

Imperial/Metric
1 young rabbit
2 tablespoons plain flour
1 teaspoon salt
2 tablespoons oil
6 oz./175 g. button onions
15 oz./425 g. can game soup
½ pint/3 dl. stock
1 bay leaf
salt and pepper
2 teaspoons cornflour
15 oz./284 g. can flageolets

American
1 young rabbit
2 tablespoons all-purpose
   flour
1 teaspoon salt
3 tablespoons oil
6 oz. button onions
15 oz. can game soup
1¼ cups stock
1 bay leaf
salt and pepper
2 teaspoons cornstarch
15 oz. can green beans

Joint the rabbit and coat the joints in the flour mixed with the salt. Fry in one tablespoon of the oil until golden brown. Lift out into a casserole and fry the onions in the remaining oil. Add the onions, soup, stock, bay leaf, salt, pepper and the liquid from the canned flageolets, to the rabbit. Cover and bake in a moderately hot oven (375°F, 190°C, Gas Mark 5) for 1 hour and 30 minutes. Remove the rabbit joints. Mix the cornflour with a little cold water and stir into the liquid in the casserole. Put back rabbit joints, pour sauce over the rabbit and add the beans. Return to the oven for 15 minutes. Serves 4-6.

Tuna Tetrazzini

Imperial/Metric
1 small onion
2 sticks celery
1½ oz./40 g. butter
2 tablespoons plain flour
½ teaspoon salt
pinch pepper
¼ teaspoon Worcestershire
 sauce
½ pint/3 dl. milk
4 oz./125 g. spaghetti
4 oz./125 g. mushrooms
6½ oz./184 g. can tuna fish
2 tablespoons grated
 Parmesan cheese
2 tablespoons sliced green
 olives

American
1 small onion
2 stalks celery
3 tablespoons butter
2 tablespoons all-purpose
 flour
½ teaspoon salt
dash pepper
¼ teaspoon Worcestershire
 sauce
1¼ cups milk
4 oz. spaghetti
1 cup mushrooms
7 oz. can tuna fish
2 tablespoons grated
 Parmesan cheese
2 tablespoons sliced green
 olives

Chop the onion and celery finely and sauté in 1 oz./25 g. of the butter until soft. Stir in the flour, seasonings and Worcestershire sauce. Cook for 2-3 minutes. Gradually add the milk, stirring until thickened. Cook the spaghetti in boiling salted water until tender. Drain well and mix with the sauce. Slice the mushrooms and fry in the remaining butter. Drain the tuna fish. Alternate layers of the spaghetti mixture, tuna and mushrooms in a lightly greased 2 pint/generous 1 litre/1½ quart casserole, ending with a layer of spaghetti. Sprinkle the cheese and sliced olives on top. Bake in a moderate oven (350°F, 180°C, Gas Mark 4) for 30 minutes.

Devils on horseback

Imperial/Metric
2 tablespoons French
 mustard
pinch cayenne pepper
few drops Tabasco sauce
8 rashers streaky bacon
16 shelled oysters

American
2 tablespoons French
 mustard
pinch cayenne pepper
few drops Tabasco sauce
8 slices side bacon
16 shelled oysters

Mix the mustard with the cayenne pepper and Tabasco sauce. Spread thinly on one side of the bacon slices. Cut each bacon rasher in half. Wrap each piece of bacon around an oyster with the mustard on the inside. Secure with a wooden pick or skewer. Grill for 10 minutes or until the bacon is crisp. Or, bake in a hot oven (450°F, 230°C, Gas Mark 8) for 10-15 minutes. Serve on buttered toast. Serves 2 as a snack, 4 as a savoury.

Quick scalloped cauliflower

Imperial/Metric
1 small cauliflower
2 medium carrots
5½ oz./156 g. can condensed
 cream of mushroom soup
2 slices streaky bacon
2 oz./50 g. Cheddar cheese,
 grated

American
1 small cauliflower
2 medium carrots
1 small can condensed
 cream of mushroom soup
2 slices side bacon
¼ cup grated Cheddar
 cheese

Divide the cauliflower into florets. Cut the carrots into narrow strips. Cook vegetables in boiling salted water for 10 minutes. Drain, place in an ovenproof casserole dish. Pour the condensed soup over the vegetables. Fry the bacon until crisp. Drain and crumble. Sprinkle the cooked crumbled bacon and the grated cheese over the soup and vegetables. Bake in a moderate oven (350°F, 180°C, Gas Mark 4) for 20 minutes.

Vegetables and salads

Gone are the days of limp boiled cabbage and mushy Brussels sprouts. We now cook vegetables for the shortest time possible and enjoy them while still crisp and barely tender, or even raw in salads. Combined with fruit they make surprisingly delicious accompaniments to main dishes and taste good enough to be served as a separate course.

Aubergines in cream cheese

Imperial/Metric
4 medium aubergines
salt and ground black
  pepper
6 tablespoons oil
6 oz./175 g. cream cheese
$\frac{1}{4}$ pint/$1\frac{1}{2}$ dl. single cream
1 clove garlic, chopped
2 tablespoons finely
  chopped chives

American
4 medium eggplants
salt and ground black
  pepper
6 tablespoons oil
6 oz. cream cheese
$\frac{1}{2}$ cup coffee cream
1 clove garlic, chopped
2 tablespoons finely
  chopped chives

Peel the aubergines, cut in slices lengthwise, sprinkle with salt and leave to stand for 30 minutes. Rinse and dry with absorbent kitchen paper. Cook until pale golden in the oil, remove, draining them carefully, and keep hot. Beat together the cream cheese, cream, garlic, chives and freshly ground pepper to taste. Use any surplus oil to grease a shallow flameproof dish. Fill with alternate layers of aubergine and cheese mixture, ending with a layer of cheese. Place under a medium grill until well browned.

Red cabbage and carrot layer

Imperial/Metric
1 thick slice fat bacon
1 small red cabbage,
  shredded
8 oz./225 g. carrots, cut
  in thin strips
salt and pepper
$\frac{1}{4}$ pint/$1\frac{1}{2}$ dl. orange juice
$\frac{1}{2}$ oz./15 g. butter

American
1 thick slice fat bacon
1 small red cabbage,
  shredded
$\frac{1}{2}$ lb. carrots, cut in thin
  strips
salt and pepper
$\frac{1}{2}$ cup orange juice
1 tablespoon butter

Place the bacon in the bottom of a flameproof casserole, add the cabbage and julienne strips of carrot, sprinkling the layers with salt and pepper. Pour in the orange juice, arrange dots of butter on top, cover and cook over moderate heat for 20 minutes.

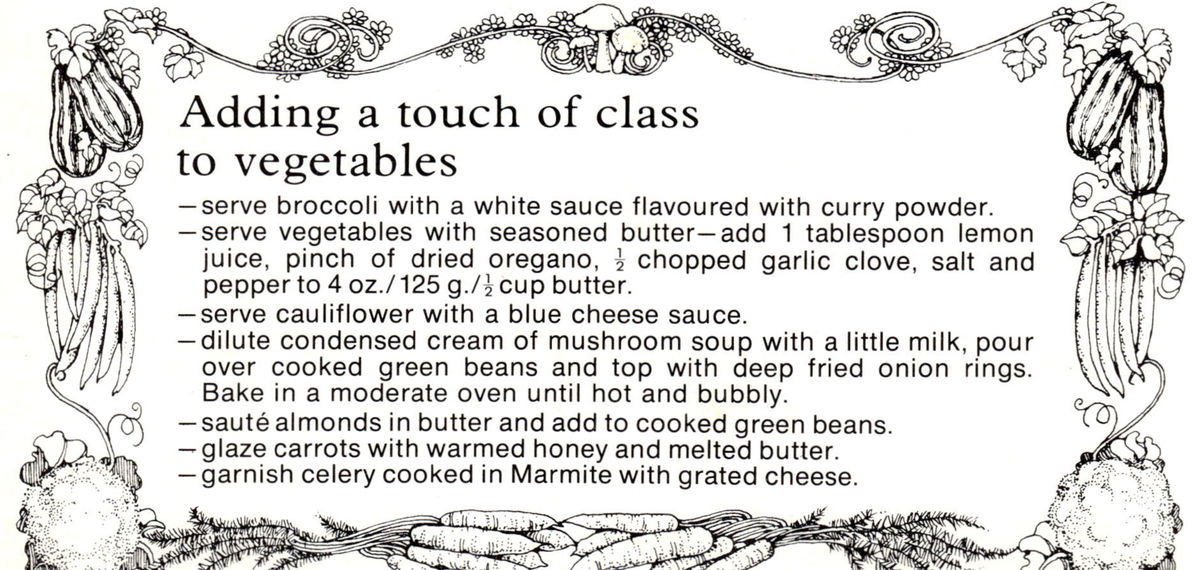

Adding a touch of class to vegetables

— serve broccoli with a white sauce flavoured with curry powder.
— serve vegetables with seasoned butter—add 1 tablespoon lemon juice, pinch of dried oregano, $\frac{1}{2}$ chopped garlic clove, salt and pepper to 4 oz./125 g./$\frac{1}{2}$ cup butter.
— serve cauliflower with a blue cheese sauce.
— dilute condensed cream of mushroom soup with a little milk, pour over cooked green beans and top with deep fried onion rings. Bake in a moderate oven until hot and bubbly.
— sauté almonds in butter and add to cooked green beans.
— glaze carrots with warmed honey and melted butter.
— garnish celery cooked in Marmite with grated cheese.

 Carrot loaf

Imperial/Metric
4 lb./2 kg. carrots
1 medium onion, grated
3 tablespoons fine semolina
2 teaspoons flour
6 eggs
1 tablespoon single cream
salt and pepper
½ teaspoon grated nutmeg
watercress to garnish

American
4 lb. carrots
1 medium onion, grated
3 tablespoons fine semolina
2 teaspoons all-purpose flour
6 eggs
1 tablespoon coffee cream
salt and pepper
½ teaspoon grated nutmeg
watercress to garnish

Slice the carrots and cook in boiling salted water until tender, then liquidise or purée and mix with the onion. Beat in the semolina, flour, lightly beaten eggs, cream, salt, pepper and nutmeg. Pour the mixture into a well greased 2 lb./1 kg. loaf tin and bake in a moderate oven (350°F, 180°C, Gas Mark 4) for 1 hour. Turn out onto a clean kitchen towel, cover with a warm serving dish and turn over. Serve sliced, garnished with watercress. Serves 8.
Note: This loaf is particularly good served with hot sliced gammon or cold ham.

Frosted Brussels sprouts with croûtons

Imperial/Metric
1 lb./450 g. Brussels
  sprouts
½ oz./15 g. butter
2 tablespoons finely
  chopped onion
1 tablespoon flour
2 teaspoons brown sugar
½ teaspoon salt
½ teaspoon dry mustard
4 fl. oz./125 ml. milk
¼ pint/1½ dl. soured cream
fried bread croûtons

American
1 lb. Brussels sprouts
1 tablespoon butter or
  margarine
2 tablespoons finely
  chopped onion
1 tablespoon all-purpose
  flour
2 teaspoons brown sugar
½ teaspoon salt
½ teaspoon dry mustard
½ cup milk
⅔ cup soured cream
croûtons

Trim the Brussels sprouts. Cook them in boiling salted water until tender. While the sprouts are cooking, melt the butter in a saucepan. Add the onion and cook until limp, but not brown. Stir in the flour, brown sugar, salt and dry mustard. Cook for 1 minute. Gradually add the milk and cook, stirring constantly, until the sauce thickens and boils. Remove from the heat. Stir in the soured cream. Drain the cooked Brussels sprouts. Pour the soured cream sauce over the sprouts. Reheat, but do not allow to boil. Garnish with croûtons.

Herb-roasted corn cobs

Imperial/Metric
2 oz./50 g. butter
½ teaspoon dried marjoram
½ teaspoon dried rosemary
4 cobs sweetcorn
8 outer cabbage leaves

American
¼ cup butter or margarine
½ teaspoon dried marjoram
½ teaspoon dried rosemary
4 corn cobs
8 outer cabbage leaves

Beat the butter with the herbs. Remove the husks from the corn cobs. Spread the herbed butter on each corn cob. Place 4 cabbage leaves in a lightly greased shallow baking dish. Arrange the corn cobs on top of the cabbage leaves and cover them with the remaining cabbage leaves. Cover tightly with foil, sealing well, and bake in a hot oven (425°F, 220°C, Gas Mark 7) for 25-30 minutes. Discard cabbage leaves.

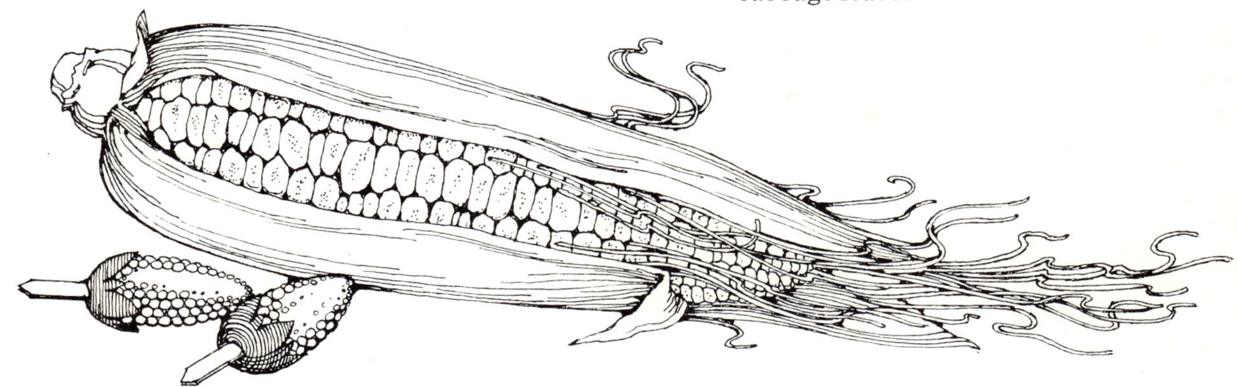

Sherried onion rings

Imperial/Metric
3 medium onions
½ teaspoon salt
¼ teaspoon freshly ground
  black pepper
2 oz./50 g. butter
2 fl. oz./50 ml. dry sherry
2 tablespoons flaked
  almonds

American
3 medium onions
½ teaspoon salt
¼ teaspoon freshly ground
  black pepper
¼ cup butter or margarine
¼ cup cooking sherry
2 tablespoons flaked
  almonds

Slice the onions and separate them into rings. Season with salt and pepper. Melt the butter in a large frying pan. Toss the onion rings in the melted butter. Cook until tender, but not browned. Add the sherry and cook for a further 2-3 minutes, then stir in the flaked almonds. Serve with grilled steak or fried chicken.

Celery in rich tomato

Imperial/Metric
2 heads celery
15 oz./425 g. can whole
  tomatoes
2 tablespoons tomato
  ketchup
1 medium onion, grated
2 bay leaves
salt and pepper
butter
4 oz./125 g. Cheddar
  cheese, grated

American
2 heads celery
2 cups canned whole
  tomatoes
2 tablespoons tomato
  catsup
1 medium onion, grated
2 bay leaves
salt and pepper
butter
1 cup grated Cheddar
  cheese

Trim the tops and outer stalks from the celery and cut each head in half. Cook gently, covered, in boiling salted water until just tender. Meanwhile, clean and finely chop one or two outer stalks of celery. Cook with the canned tomatoes, tomato ketchup, onion and bay leaves for about 15 minutes, or until mixture is considerably reduced and thickened. Season to taste. Remove bay leaves. Butter a shallow ovenproof dish, place the well-drained celery halves in this, sprinkle with half the cheese, cover with the tomato mixture and sprinkle over remaining cheese. Place under a medium grill until cheese turns golden.

Orange 'n lemon beetroot

Imperial/Metric
2 lb./1 kg. fresh beetroot
2 tablespoons lemon juice
2 fl. oz./50 ml. orange
   juice
1 tablespoon wine vinegar
1 tablespoon clear honey
1 tablespoon cornflour
$\frac{1}{2}$ teaspoon salt
pinch pepper
2 oz./50 g. butter
$\frac{1}{2}$ teaspoon grated lemon
   zest
$\frac{1}{2}$ teaspoon grated orange
   zest

American
2 lb. fresh beets
2 tablespoons lemon juice
$\frac{1}{4}$ cup orange juice
1 tablespoon wine vinegar
1 tablespoon clear honey
1 tablespoon cornstarch
$\frac{1}{2}$ teaspoon salt
pinch pepper
$\frac{1}{4}$ cup butter or margarine
$\frac{1}{2}$ teaspoon grated lemon
   rind
$\frac{1}{2}$ teaspoon grated orange
   rind

Cook the beetroot in boiling water until tender, about 50 minutes. Peel and cut into $\frac{1}{2}$ inch/1 cm. dice. Combine the lemon juice, orange juice, vinegar, honey and cornflour. Bring to the boil and cook over medium heat until the sauce is thick and clear. Remove from heat. Add the diced beetroot, salt, pepper and butter. Heat through. Pour into a serving dish and garnish with the grated orange and lemon rind.

Walnut side salad

Imperial/Metric
1 oz./25 g. seedless raisins
2 tablespoons French
   dressing
4 slices mild onion
1 large tomato
1 lb./450 g. white cabbage
2 oz./50 g. walnut
   halves

American
2 tablespoons seedless
   raisins
3 tablespoons Italian
   dressing
4 slices mild onion
1 large tomato
1 lb. white cabbage
$\frac{1}{2}$ cup walnut halves

Soak the raisins in the salad dressing for 2 hours, until plumped. Break each slice of onion carefully into rings and finely slice the tomato. Shred the cabbage finely into a bowl and toss with the walnut halves, raisins and dressing. Divide between four individual salad bowls, top with tomato slices and onion rings.

Courgette salad

Imperial/Metric
8 oz./225 g. courgettes
2 teaspoons lemon juice
4 oz./100 g. button
  mushrooms
3 tablespoons French
  dressing
green salad

American
½ lb. zucchini
2 teaspoons lemon juice
1 cup button mushrooms
4 tablespoons Italian
  dressing
green salad

Slice the courgettes thinly and blanch for 2 minutes in boiling salted water. Drain well and sprinkle with half the lemon juice. Slice the mushrooms as thinly and toss in 2 tablespoons hot courgette water over moderate heat for 1 minute. Drain well and sprinkle with the remaining lemon juice. When completely cold, combine with the salad dressing and chill in a covered dish for at least 1 hour. Serve on a bed of green salad.

Sweetcorn and crab salad

Imperial/Metric
1 small red pepper
1 large cooked crab
4 oz./125 g. cooked long
  grain rice
2 tablespoons mayonnaise
8 oz./225 g. cooked
  sweetcorn kernels
1 tablespoon chopped
  chives
dressing:
2 tablespoons lemon juice
½ teaspoon salt
¼ teaspoon white pepper
½ teaspoon castor sugar
4 tablespoons corn oil

American
1 small red pepper
1 large cooked crab
1 cup cooked long grain
  rice
2 tablespoons mayonnaise
1 cup cooked corn kernels
1 tablespoon chopped
  chives
dressing:
2 tablespoons lemon juice
½ teaspoon salt
¼ teaspoon white pepper
½ teaspoon granulated
  sugar
4 tablespoons corn oil

First make the dressing. Beat together the lemon juice, seasoning and sugar and gradually add the oil. Deseed and cut the pepper into strips. Marinate in the dressing for at least 2 hours. Remove the flesh from the crab and reserve the claw meat. Mix the remaining crab meat lightly with the rice and mayonnaise and place in a shallow serving dish. Toss the chunks of claw meat, corn kernels, red pepper strips and chives together in the dressing and arrange over the rice mixture. Serve chilled.

Sweets

Within this mouth-watering category come hot puddings, creamy cold desserts and pretty cakes. The recipes sound and taste so good! Cheesecakes are becoming increasingly popular; try my Marbled pumpkin or Damson cheesecake. For a touch of excitement, use exotic fruits like figs and Chinese gooseberries, home grown or imported, combined in a colourful salad with cider or wine.

Pineapple ginger pudding

Imperial Metric
4 oz./125 g. butter or
  margarine
4 oz./125 g. castor sugar
2 large eggs
6 oz./175 g. self-raising
  flour
1 teaspoon baking powder
pinch salt
3 tablespoons canned
  pineapple juice
2 tablespoons ginger
  marmalade

American
½ cup butter or margarine
½ cup granulated sugar
2 large eggs
1½ cups all-purpose flour
2½ teaspoons baking
  powder
pinch salt
3 tablespoons canned
  pineapple juice
2 tablespoons ginger
  marmalade

Beat together the butter and sugar until light and fluffy. Gradually beat in the eggs and a little of the flour. Sieve the remaining flour with the baking powder and salt. Fold into the batter. Stir in 2 tablespoons pineapple juice. Grease a 2 pint/generous 1 litre pudding basin and spoon the ginger marmalade mixed with the remaining tablespoon of pineapple juice into the base. Fill the pudding basin with the batter and cover with greaseproof paper. Steam, tightly covered, for 2 hours. Turn out and serve with the pineapple sauce. Serves 4-6.

Pineapple sauce

Imperial/Metric
2 teaspoons cornflour
½ pint/3 dl. canned
    pineapple juice
zest and juice of ½ lemon
1 tablespoon butter

American
2 teaspoons cornstarch
1¼ cups canned
    pineapple juice
rind and juice of ½ lemon
1 tablespoon butter

Mix the cornflour with two tablespoons of the pineapple juice. Bring the remaining juice to the boil and stir in the cornflour paste. Stir in the lemon zest and juice. Cook and stir until thick and smooth, about 2-3 minutes. Beat in the butter. Serve over Pineapple ginger pudding.

Toasted apple pudding with brandied cream

Imperial/Metric
4 slices white bread
2 eggs
4 oz./125 g. castor sugar
1 teaspoon ground
    cinnamon
¼ teaspoon salt
1 teaspoon vanilla essence
½ pint/3 dl. milk
8 oz./225 g. apple purée
1 oz./25 g. butter or
    margarine, melted
1 egg white
1 tablespoon clear honey
¼ pint/1½ dl. double cream
2 tablespoons brandy

American
4 slices white bread
2 eggs
½ cup granulated sugar
1 teaspoon ground
    cinnamon
¼ teaspoon salt
1 teaspoon vanilla extract
1¼ cups milk
1 cup applesauce
2 tablespoons butter or
    margarine, melted
1 egg white
1 tablespoon clear honey
⅔ cup whipping cream
2 tablespoons brandy

Toast the bread lightly. Cut into ½ inch/ 1 cm. strips. Beat the eggs lightly; stir in the sugar, cinnamon, salt, vanilla, milk, apple purée and butter. Place one third of the toasted bread strips in a baking dish. Cover with half of the apple mixture. Repeat another layer of bread strips and the remaining apple mixture. Top with remaining bread strips, making a lattice pattern. Bake in a moderate oven (325°F, 170°C or Gas Mark 3) for one hour or until the centre is set. Meanwhile to make the brandied cream, whisk the egg white until stiff. Gradually whisk the honey into the egg white. Whip the double cream and fold into the beaten egg white. Stir in the brandy. Serve the pudding warm with the sauce. Serves 6.

Blackberry and pear pudding

Imperial/Metric
8 oz./225 g. plain flour
½ teaspoon salt
1 teaspoon sugar
4 fl. oz./125 ml. milk
1 teaspoon dried yeast
2 oz./50 g. butter
2 eggs
3 medium pears
1 tablespoon castor sugar
8 oz./225 g. blackberries

American
2 cups all-purpose flour
½ teaspoon salt
1 teaspoon sugar
½ cup milk
1 teaspoon dried yeast
¼ cup butter
2 eggs
3 medium pears
1 tablespoon granulated
    sugar
½ lb. blackberries

Sieve the flour and salt together into a bowl. Dissolve the sugar in the warm milk and sprinkle the dried yeast on top. Leave for about 10 minutes, or until frothy. Melt the butter and beat the yeast mixture into the flour, work in the melted butter and the lightly beaten eggs to give a soft dough. Allow to rise, covered, in a warm place until doubled in bulk. Meanwhile, peel, quarter and core the pears, and roll in the castor sugar. Butter a loose-bottomed 8 inch/20 cm. cake tin or deep flan tin, knock back the risen dough and shape to fit the tin, leaving a raised edge. Fill the centre with the pears. Bake in a moderately hot oven (375°F, 190°C, Gas Mark 5) for 30-40 minutes. Test that the dough is cooked by inserting the blade of a knife which should come out clean. Remove from the oven, unmould, sprinkle with the blackberries and serve warm with whipped cream, if liked.

 Figs with almond stuffing

Imperial/Metric
8 large figs
2 oz./50 g. ground almonds
2 oz./50 g. icing sugar
1 small Petit Suisse cheese
8 whole almonds

American
8 large figs
½ cup ground almonds
¼ cup confectioner's sugar
2 tablespoons cream cheese
8 whole almonds

Cut the figs in half almost through to the base and again at right angles, so that they open out into four 'petals'. Beat together the ground almonds, sieved icing sugar and the cheese. Fill the centres of the figs with this mixture and decorate with whole almonds.

Exotic fruit salad

Imperial/Metric
4 fresh figs
2 Chinese gooseberries
8 oz./225 g. green grapes
2 crisp apples
2 pears
2 tablespoons lemon juice
1 pomegranate
2 tangerines
35.2 fl. oz./1 litre bottle
  dry cider

American
4 fresh figs
2 Kiwi fruits
$\frac{1}{2}$ lb. green grapes
2 crisp apples
2 pears
2 tablespoons lemon juice
1 pomegranate
2 tangerines
$4\frac{1}{2}$ cups cider

Slice the figs; peel and slice the Chinese gooseberries. Peel and remove the seeds from the green grapes. Slice the apples, leaving the peel on. Peel and slice the pears. Sprinkle the lemon juice on the apples and pears to prevent discolouring. Cut the pomegranate into small pieces. Peel and segment the tangerines, removing the seeds. Combine the prepared fruits and cover with the dry cider. Chill until serving time. Serves 8.

Blueberry pancake layer

Imperial/Metric
4 oz./125 g. plain flour
¼ teaspoon salt
2 eggs
½ pint/3 dl. milk
1 tablespoon melted fat
2 10 oz./283 g. cans
 blueberries
1 tablespoon cornflour
zest and juice of 1 lemon
½ pint/3 dl. double cream

American
1 cup all-purpose flour
¼ teaspoon salt
2 eggs
1¼ cups milk
1 tablespoon melted
 shortening
2½ cups canned blueberries
1 tablespoon cornstarch
rind and juice of 1 lemon
1¼ cups whipping cream

To make the pancakes, sieve the flour and salt into a bowl. Make a well in the centre and beat in the eggs and a little of the milk. Gradually beat in the remaining milk and the melted fat. Beat for 3-4 minutes. Lightly oil a frying pan. Use 2 tablespoons batter for each pancake, fry golden brown on both sides. Stack them on a tea towel. Continue to make the pancakes until the batter is finished. Drain the blueberries, reserving the syrup. Mix 2 tablespoons of the syrup with the cornflour and bring the remainder to the boil. Stir in the cornflour paste, lemon zest and juice. Cook and stir over low heat until thickened. Cool. Place a pancake on a serving dish. Whip the cream until stiff. Spread some over the pancake and scatter with some drained blueberries. Repeat until all the pancakes are used. Chill and serve in wedges with the prepared blueberry sauce poured over. Serves 6.

Note: If fresh blueberries are available, cook in water with sugar to sweeten until soft, and use juice as above.

Fresh lime mousse

Imperial/Metric
1 packet lime jelly
½ pint/3 dl. hot water
15 oz./425 g. can
  evaporated milk
zest and juice of 2 fresh
  limes
¼ pint/1½ dl. double cream

American
3 oz. package lime-flavored
  gelatin
1¼ cups hot water
15 oz. can evaporated milk
2 fresh limes, rind and
  juice
½ cup whipping cream

Dissolve the jelly in the water and stir in the evaporated milk, lime zest and juice (set aside a little zest for decoration). Pour the mixture into a dampened mould and refrigerate until set. Turn out on to a plate. Whisk the cream until stiff and pipe around the jelly. Sprinkle with the lime zest.

Blackberry and apple coupes

Imperial/Metric
1 packet Knorr Apple Sauce
  mix, or ½ pint/3 dl. sweet
  apple purée
1 oz./25 g. chopped toasted
  almonds or hazelnuts
¼ pint/1½ dl. double cream
1 egg white
1 lb./450 g. fresh black-
  berries or raspberries

American
1¼ cups applesauce,
  sweetened
¼ cup chopped toasted
  almonds or hazelnuts
½ cup whipping cream
1 egg white
1 lb. fresh blackberries
  or raspberries

Make up the sauce as directed on the packet. Stir in the nuts. Whip the cream, place a little in a piping bag for decoration and fold the remainder into the apple mixture. Whisk the egg white until stiff and fold into the apple cream. Arrange layers of blackberries and apple cream in glass dishes and decorate with whipped cream.

Chocolate cups with ginger cream

Imperial/Metric
8 oz./225 g. plain chocolate
4 pieces stem ginger
1 tablespoon ginger syrup
¼ pint/1½ dl. double cream
chopped pistachio nuts
  to decorate

American
½ lb. chocolate
4 pieces stem ginger
1 tablespoon ginger syrup
½ cup whipping cream
chopped pistachio nuts
  to decorate

Melt the chocolate in a basin over a pan of hot water. Using the back of a teaspoon, coat the insides of paper bun cases with a layer of melted chocolate then chill until set. Repeat twice until the cases are evenly coated. Remove the paper cases. Chop three pieces of ginger, mix with the ginger syrup and divide between the chocolate cups. Whip the cream until thick and place in a piping bag fitted with a star nozzle. Pipe a rosette of cream into each chocolate cup and sprinkle lightly with chopped pistachio nuts. Slice the remaining piece of ginger and use to decorate rosettes. Chill for up to 2 hours and serve immediately on removing from the refrigerator.

Grapes in nectar

Imperial/Metric
8 oz./225 g. green grapes
8 oz./225 g. black grapes
1 teaspoon lemon juice
4 tablespoons clear honey
2 tablespoons sweet sherry
1 oz./25 g. flaked almonds,
  toasted

American
½ lb. green grapes
½ lb. purple grapes
1 teaspoon lemon juice
5 tablespoons clear honey
3 tablespoons sweet sherry
¼ cup slivered toasted
  almonds

Halve and deseed the grapes and place in a basin. Mix together the lemon juice, honey and sherry and pour over the grapes. Allow to stand at room temperature for at least 2 hours, then chill until required. Spoon into tall glasses and decorate each with a sprinkling of toasted flaked almonds.

# Apple and chestnut charlotte

Imperial/Metric
26 boudoir biscuits
4 tablespoons dry sherry
¼ pint/1½ dl. chestnut purée
½ pint/3 dl. apple purée
½ pint/3 dl. double cream,
  whipped
marrons glacés for
  decoration

American
26 ladyfingers
4 tablespoons dry sherry
generous ½ cup chestnut purée
generous ½ cup applesauce
1¼ cups whipping cream,
  whipped
marrons glacés for
  decoration

Dip 2 boudoir biscuits in the sherry and place in the bottom of a Tupperware Jel 'n' serve. Dip 16 more biscuits and arrange in the mould filling the curves. Mix together the chestnut purée and the apple purée and put half into the mould. Then add half the whipped cream and top with four biscuits. Add remaining purée and cream (reserving a little for decoration) and finish with a layer of biscuits. Seal the mould and press firmly. Chill. To serve remove the seal and turn the charlotte on to a serving dish. Remove the design seal and lift off the mould. Decorate with the reserved cream and marrons glacés. An 8 inch/20 cm. spring-sided or loose-bottomed mould could be substituted, spacing out the biscuits evenly. Serves 8.

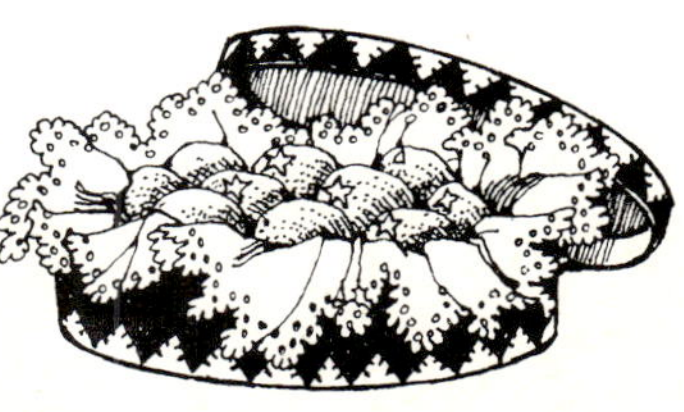

Grape and coconut flan

Imperial/Metric
3 eggs
3 oz./75 g. castor sugar
3 oz./75 g. plain flour
1 oz./25 g. butter, melted
filling:
4 tablespoons grated fresh
  coconut
8 oz./225 g. apricot jam
3 oz./75 g. green grapes
3 oz./75 g. black grapes
grated fresh coconut to
  decorate

American
3 eggs
$\frac{1}{3}$ cup granulated sugar
$\frac{3}{4}$ cup all-purpose flour
2 tablespoons butter,
  melted
filling:
4 tablespoons grated fresh
  coconut
$\frac{1}{2}$ cup apricot jam
$\frac{1}{2}$ cup seedless green
  grapes
$\frac{1}{2}$ cup Tokay grapes
grated fresh coconut to
  decorate

To make the flan case, whisk the eggs and sugar together over a bowl of hot water until thick and the whisk leaves a trail when lifted from the mixture. Remove from the heat and continue whisking until cold. Fold in the flour and butter until well blended. Turn mixture into a greased 8 inch/20 cm. flan tin and bake in a moderately hot oven (375°F, 190°C, Gas Mark 5) for 20 minutes. Cool on a wire rack. To make the filling, mix the coconut with three-quarters of the jam and spread in the base of the flan case. Halve the grapes and remove the pips. Fill the flan case decoratively with the halved grapes. Sieve the remaining apricot jam and heat in a small pan with 1 tablespoon water. Use this glaze to brush over the grapes and decorate the top with a little more grated coconut.

Damson cheesecake

Imperial/Metric	**American**
4 oz./100 g. butter	$\frac{1}{2}$ cup butter
8 oz./225 g. digestive biscuits, crushed	$\frac{1}{2}$ lb. Graham crackers, crushed
8 oz./225 g. sugar	1 cup sugar
8 oz./225 g. damsons	$\frac{1}{2}$ lb. damsons
$\frac{1}{4}$ pint/1$\frac{1}{2}$ dl. water	$\frac{2}{3}$ cup water
filling:	filling:
1 lb./450 g. cream cheese	2 cups cream cheese
4 eggs, separated	4 eggs, separated
4 tablespoons lemon juice	$\frac{1}{3}$ cup lemon juice
grated zest of $\frac{1}{2}$ lemon	grated rind of $\frac{1}{2}$ lemon
1 tablespoon gelatine	1 tablespoon gelatin
6 tablespoons cold water	$\frac{1}{2}$ cup cold water
4 tablespoons sugar	5 tablespoons sugar
4 tablespoons double cream	$\frac{1}{3}$ cup heavy cream

Melt the butter and stir into the biscuit crumbs with 4 oz./100 g. of the sugar. Press this to the base and sides of a well-greased deep plain flan tin and place in a moderately hot oven (400°F, 200°C, Gas Mark 6) for 10 minutes. Cool. Halve and stone the damsons. Place the water and remaining sugar in a saucepan and allow sugar to dissolve over gentle heat. Use the syrup to poach the damsons gently for 20 minutes and cool in the syrup. Drain the damsons and arrange in the base of the flan case. To make the filling, soften the cream cheese and beat until smooth. Gradually beat in the egg yolks then the lemon juice and zest. Allow the gelatine to dissolve in the water in a basin over a pan of hot water then stir into the cheese mixture. Beat the egg whites stiffly and gradually beat in the sugar. Whip the cream. Fold the meringue and whipped cream into the cheese mixture alternately. Spoon the cheesecake mixture over the damsons, smooth the top and chill well. Dip in hot water and lift the cheesecake onto a serving dish.

Marbled pumpkin cheesecake

Imperial/Metric	**American**
10 digestive biscuits	1 cup Graham wafer crumbs
1 oz./25 g. demerara sugar	2 tablespoons brown sugar
2 oz./50 g. butter, melted	$\frac{1}{4}$ cup melted butter
1 lb./450 g. pumpkin	1 lb. pumpkin or 1 cup canned pumpkin
6 oz./175 g. cream cheese	6 oz. cream cheese
4 fl. oz./125 ml. milk	$\frac{1}{2}$ cup milk
4 oz./125 g. castor sugar	$\frac{1}{2}$ cup granulated sugar
2 egg yolks	2 egg yolks
1 tablespoon flour	1 tablespoon all-purpose flour
1 teaspoon vanilla essence	1 teaspoon vanilla extract
1 teaspoon ground cinnamon	1 teaspoon ground cinnamon
$\frac{1}{4}$ teaspoon ground nutmeg	$\frac{1}{4}$ teaspoon ground nutmeg
pinch salt	dash salt
2 egg whites	2 egg whites
topping:	topping:
4 fl. oz. 125 ml. soured cream	$\frac{1}{2}$ cup soured cream
1 tablespoon sugar	1 tablespoon granulated sugar
$\frac{1}{2}$ teaspoon ground cinnamon	$\frac{1}{2}$ teaspoon ground cinnamon

Crush the digestive biscuits. Mix the crumbs with the demerara sugar and melted butter. Press into a large loose bottomed cake tin. Bake in a moderate oven (325°F, 170°C, Gas Mark 3) for 8 minutes. Peel and remove the seeds from the pumpkin. Steam until tender, then mash until smooth and set aside. Soften the cream cheese. Beat in the milk, sugar, egg yolks, flour, vanilla and spices. Whisk the egg whites with the salt until stiff. Fold into the cream cheese mixture. Swirl the mashed pumpkin through the cream cheese mixture. Turn into the prepared crumb crust. Bake in a moderate oven (325°F, 170°C, Gas Mark 3) for 1 hour. Combine the soured cream, sugar and cinnamon. Spread over the cheesecake and bake 5 minutes longer. Chill thoroughly before serving. Serves 12.

Topaz ring cake

Imperial/Metric
4 oz./125 g. castor sugar
4 oz./125 g. soft margarine
4 oz./125 g. self-raising
  flour
2 eggs
1 teaspoon baking powder
grated zest of 1 lemon

American
½ cup granulated sugar
½ cup soft margarine
1 cup all-purpose flour
2 eggs
2 teaspoons baking powder
grated rind of 1 lemon

Grease a 7 inch/18 cm. ring mould. Beat all the ingredients together until well blended, about 2 minutes. Spread the batter evenly in the ring mould and bake in a moderate oven (350°F, 180°C, Gas Mark 4) for 25-30 minutes. Leave in the mould for 5 minutes, then turn out on a wire cooling tray. Ice with lemon-treacle icing and decorate with caramel diamonds and grapes, see recipe below.

Lemon-treacle icing and caramel diamonds

Imperial/Metric
10 oz./275 g. icing sugar
4 oz./125 g. butter
1 tablespoon treacle
3 tablespoons lemon juice
4 oz./125 g. castor sugar
¼ pint/1½ dl. water
few black and green
  grapes

American
2½ cups confectioner's
  sugar
½ cup butter
1 tablespoon light molasses
3 tablespoons lemon juice
½ cup granulated sugar
½ cup water
few purple and green
  grapes

Beat the icing sugar with the butter until light and fluffy. Add the treacle to two tablespoons of the creamed mixture. Beat the lemon juice into the remaining mixture. Cut the cake in half horizontally and spread the treacle icing over the bottom half. Replace the top half and spread the lemon icing over the cake. To make the caramel diamonds, boil the castor sugar and water in a small saucepan until a pale golden colour. Pour into an oiled baking tray and leave to harden. Cut into diamond shapes and arrange around the cake. Fill the centre of the cake with black and green grapes.

Pickles and preserves

Try something new this year as a complete change from your usual mixed pickles and tomato sauce. Imagination is the essential ingredient used in devising these recipes to bring excitement to your table all the rest of the year. For instance, when the family devours the delicate pink flesh of watermelons, reserve the rind for a most unusual pickle—the recipe is here in this section.

Nine day cucumber pickles

Imperial/Metric
4 lb./2 kg. cucumbers
4 oz./125 g. salt
1½ pints—scant 1 litre
 boiling water
3 lb./1½ kg. granulated sugar
1½ pints/scant 1 litre white
 vinegar
2 teaspoons celery seed
4 cinnamon sticks

American
4 lb. cucumbers
½ cup pickling salt
4 cups boiling water
6 cups sugar
4 cups white vinegar
2 teaspoons celery seed
4 cinnamon sticks

Cover the cucumbers with the salt and water. After three days, drain off the salt water, and cover the cucumbers with cold water. Let stand 24 hours. Drain and repeat this process the 2 following days. On the seventh day, drain and slice the cucumbers in 2 inch/5 cm. lengths. Combine the sugar, vinegar, celery seed and cinnamon sticks. Bring to the boil and pour over the cucumber slices. Let stand 24 hours. Drain and reheat the liquid and pour over the cucumber slices. Let the cucumber cool in the liquid for 24 hours. On the ninth day, drain and reheat the liquid again. Place the cucumber in hot clean jars and pour the hot liquid up to the top of each jar. Seal. Place the sealed jars in a bath of boiling water and boil for 5 minutes.

Make 2 pints/generous 1 litre/5 cups.

Spicy watermelon rind pickles

Imperial/Metric
2 lb./1 kg. watermelon rind
2 oz./50 g. salt
1¾ pints/1 litre water
1 cinnamon stick
1 tablespoon whole cloves
2 lb./1 kg. granulated
 sugar
¾ pint/4 dl. white vinegar

American
2 lb. watermelon rind
¼ cup pickling salt
4¼ cups water
1 cinnamon stick
1 tablespoon whole cloves
4 cups sugar
2 cups white vinegar

Remove the dark green and pink parts from the watermelon rind; cut the pale green parts into cubes. Combine the salt and water. Soak the cubed watermelon rind in the salted water overnight. Next day, drain and rinse the watermelon rind in cold water. In a large saucepan, cover the watermelon rind with cold water. Bring to the boil and simmer for 15 minutes. Tie the spices in a muslin bag and add to the watermelon rind with the sugar and vinegar. Simmer until thick and clear. Remove muslin bag. Pour into hot clean jars and seal.

Makes 1½ pints/scant 1 litre/4 cups.

Apple and sage jelly

Imperial/Metric
2 lb./1 kg. cooking apples
2 pints/generous 1 litre
   water
1 lemon
2 lb./1 kg. granulated sugar
1 tablespoon freshly
   chopped sage
few drops green food
   colouring

American
2 lb. baking apples
5 cups water
1 lemon
4 cups sugar
1 tablespoon freshly
   chopped sage
few drops green food
   coloring

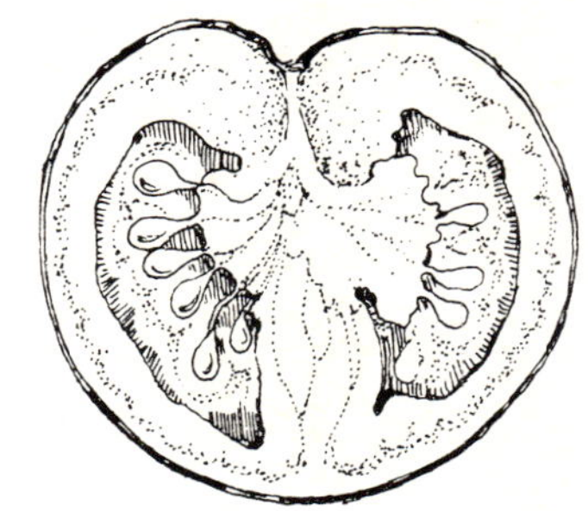

Quarter the apples and simmer in the water with the
rind from the lemon, reserving the juice, for 30 minutes
or until very tender. Pour the pulp into a jelly bag or a
piece of muslin: suspend it over a container and allow
the juice to drip overnight. Boil the juice with the
sugar and the juice from the lemon for 30 minutes.
Add the chopped sage, boil for 2 minutes, then add the
food colouring. Strain into clean jars and seal.

Makes 2½ lb./1 kg. jelly.

Green tomato marmalade

Imperial/Metric
4 lb./2 kg. green tomatoes
2 lemons
2 oranges
2 lb./1 kg. granulated sugar

American
4 lb. green tomatoes
2 lemons
2 oranges
4 cups sugar

Slice the tomatoes. Cut the lemons and oranges into
very thin slices, discarding the seeds. Place in a heavy
saucepan and cook over very low heat, stirring frequently, until thick, about 40 minutes. Add sugar,
continue cooking, stirring occasionally, for 15 minutes.
Pour into hot clean jars and seal.

Makes 2 pints/generous 1 litre/5 cups.

Spiced tomato butter

Imperial/Metric
5 lb./2½ kg. ripe tomatoes
1 small onion
12 fl. oz./350 ml. vinegar
1 lb./450 g. white sugar
12 oz./350 g. brown sugar
½ teaspoon ground cinna-
   mon
½ teaspoon ground cloves
1 teaspoon ground allspice
2 teaspoons salt

American
5 lb. ripe tomatoes
1 small onion
1½ cups vinegar
2 cups granulated sugar
1½ cups brown sugar
½ teaspoon ground
   cinnamon
½ teaspoon ground cloves
1 teaspoon ground allspice
2 teaspoons salt

Mince the tomatoes and onion, or liquidise in a
blender. Combine vinegar, sugars, spices and salt in a
heavy saucepan. Bring to the boil, add the tomato
purée and simmer over low heat until thick, stirring
frequently. Pour into hot clean jars and seal.

Makes about 4 pints/2 litres/9 cups.

Fig conserve

Imperial/Metric
3 lb./1½ kg. green figs
granulated sugar
2 fl. oz./50 ml. water

American
3 lb. green figs
sugar
¼ cup water

Remove the stalks and any damaged parts from the figs, cut in quarters. Weigh and place with the same quantity of sugar and the water in a preserving pan. Cook over gentle heat, removing scum carefully, until fruit is tender and setting point is reached. Cool for 10 minutes, stir to distribute the fruit evenly, then pour into clean warm jars and cover tightly. The same recipe can be used with other very sweet fruits which have a low pectin content and consequently poor setting qualities.

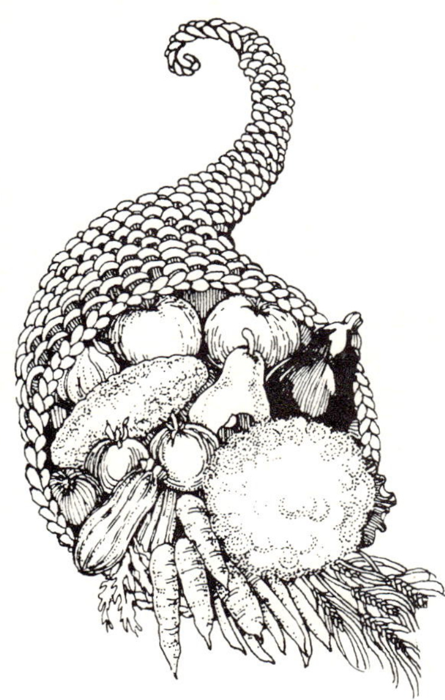

Seasonal home freezing

During the autumn months some of the most delicious and exciting vegetables are available. It is good to serve and enjoy them when they are in season, but it is even more rewarding to be able to store them in the freezer for use during the following months. However much you enjoy your runner beans and courgettes from the garden you do not want to eat them every day simply to use up the crop.

Tomatoes which are not quite perfect are ideal for sauces. The damaged parts can be cut out and a herb-flavoured sauce such as the one given in the recipe below can be made up in quantity, without adding the cream until serving time.

This is the time of year for making pickles and chutneys. Why not make use of your freezer for storing these items? The recipe on page 85 for Uncooked tomato chutney is less trouble to prepare than the traditional one and is perfect served with cold meats and poultry—particularly the Christmas turkey.

As game has a very limited season it is an ideal candidate for the freezer. Game can be frozen as it is, or made into dishes and frozen—either way the results are good. More information on freezing it un-cooked comes on page 86.

Southern fried chicken on saffron rice

Imperial/Metric
8 oz./225 g. long grain rice
2 teaspoons salt
1 large pinch ground saffron
4 southern fried chicken portions, defrosted
sauce:
2 oz./50 g. butter
1 onion, chopped
1½ oz./40 g. flour
15 oz./428 g. can tomatoes
1 teaspoon sugar
1 teaspoon dried oregano
1 bay leaf
salt and pepper
2 tablespoons double cream
1 tablespoon chopped parsley and 1 chopped spring onion to garnish

American
1⅓ cups long grain rice
2 teaspoons salt
1 large pinch ground saffron
4 southern fried chicken portions, defrosted
sauce:
¼ cup butter
1 onion, chopped
6 tablespoons all-purpose flour
2 cups canned tomatoes
1 teaspoon sugar
1 teaspoon dried oregano
1 bay leaf
salt and pepper
2 tablespoons whipping cream
1 tablespoon chopped parsley and 1 chopped green onion to garnish

First make the sauce. Melt the butter and use to sauté the onion gently until soft but not coloured. Remove from the heat and stir in the flour. Replace over heat and gradually add the tomatoes, sugar, oregano, bay leaf, and seasoning. Bring to the boil, stirring constantly, and simmer for 5 minutes. Press through a sieve and stir in the cream. Meanwhile cook the rice in plenty of boiling salted water with the saffron added. Rinse with hot water, drain and add seasoning. At the same time, deep fry the chicken portions as directed. Place a bed of saffron rice on a hot serving dish and arrange the chicken portions on top. Reheat the sauce if necessary but do not allow to boil. Spoon sauce over the chicken and garnish with parsley and onion. Serve with fried aubergines.

Fried aubergines

Imperial/Metric
4 medium aubergines
salt and ground black pepper
2 tablespoons oil

American
4 medium eggplants
salt and ground black pepper
2 tablespoons oil

Cut the aubergines in half lengthwise, make several ½ inch/1 cm. deep slashes in each side, sprinkle cut surfaces with salt. Allow to stand for 30 minutes then dry with absorbent kitchen paper. Sprinkle with black pepper. Heat the oil and use to fry the aubergine halves gently for about 8 minutes, turning until golden brown.

Ratatouille Lavandaise

Imperial/Metric
1 lb./450 g. aubergines
salt
about 4 tablespoons olive
  oil
1 large onion, sliced
1 medium green pepper
1 medium red pepper
1 lb./450 g. courgettes
4 tomatoes
1 teaspoon dried thyme
$\frac{1}{4}$ teaspoon dried basil
salt and pepper

American
1 lb. eggplants
salt
$\frac{1}{3}$ cup olive oil
1 large onion, sliced
1 medium green sweet
  pepper
1 medium red sweet pepper
1 lb. zucchini
4 tomatoes
1 teaspoon dried thyme
$\frac{1}{4}$ teaspoon dried basil
salt and pepper

Slice the aubergines and sprinkle with salt. Leave aside for 1 hour, then drain off the liquid. Dry on absorbent paper. Heat half the oil in a large frying pan and lightly fry the sliced onion. Add the remaining oil to the pan together with the seeded and sliced peppers and sliced courgettes. Continue frying gently, turning the mixture from time to time. Add the aubergines, skinned and sliced tomatoes, herbs and seasonings. Cook for a further 20-25 minutes.

To freeze: Transfer the mixture to foil trays (or polythene containers). Allow to cool, cover with lids or seals and label.
To serve: Loosen the lids from the foil trays (or transfer the mixture from the polythene containers to an ovenproof dish) and defrost and reheat in a moderate oven (350°F, 180°C, Gas Mark 4) for about 1 hour. Serve as a starter or as a vegetable.

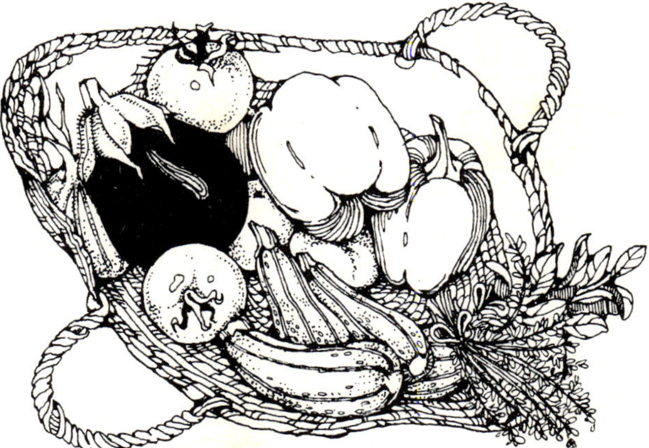

Diced cucumber with herb butter

Imperial/Metric
1 large cucumber
1 teaspoon salt
1 oz./25 g. butter
1 tablespoon chopped fresh
  herbs such as parsley,
  mint and thyme

American
1 large cucumber
1 teaspoon salt
2 tablespoons butter
1 tablespoon chopped fresh
  herbs such as parsley,
  mint and thyme

Cut the unpeeled cucumber into cubes and sprinkle with salt. Leave aside for 1 hour, then strain off the excess juices. Heat the butter in a frying pan and sauté the drained cucumber for 2 minutes over low heat. Add the chopped herbs.

To freeze: Transfer the mixture to a foil tray or polythene container. Allow to cool, cover with a lid or seal and label.
To serve: Remove the lid from the foil tray, or turn the mixture from the polythene container into an ovenproof dish. Defrost and reheat in a moderate oven (350°F, 180°C, Gas Mark 4) for 20 minutes.

Using shaped foil containers: A good tip for saving effort and time spent washing up is to pack dishes which can be defrosted and reheated in the oven in shaped foil containers. The deeper shapes come complete with a lid, which is easier to write on before you slip it into place, and secure by pressing the foil lip securely over it all round the container. Remove the lid and place the container on a baking tray in a hot oven (425°F, 220°C, Gas Mark 7) for 25-30 minutes to defrost and reheat a small size. Serve straight from the container which, if carefully washed while still warm, can be used again.

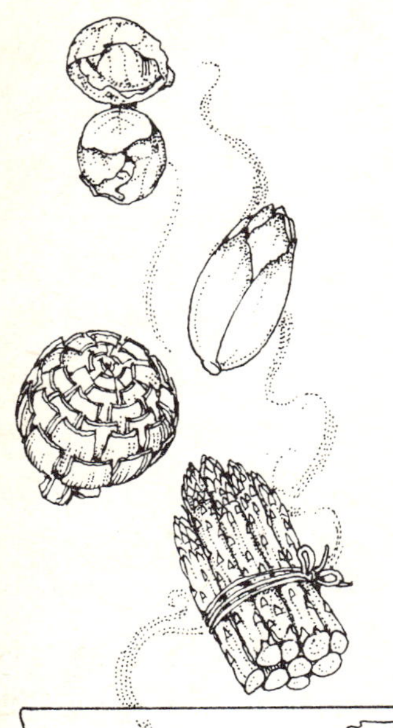

Freezing vegetables: Most vegetables, providing they have been blanched, can be stored for 12 months. The purpose of blanching vegetables prior to freezing is to destroy the enzyme action, preserve the colour, flavour and texture. It also helps preserve the Vitamin C content. When the time comes to cook frozen vegetables which have been blanched, the cooking time is less than for fresh vegetables as they have been partially cooked. To blanch vegetables: first prepare the vegetables according to type—see the following chart. Plunge the prepared vegetables, 1 lb./450 g. at a time, into a large pan containing rapidly boiling water. Keep the heat under the pan high to ensure that the vegetables and water return to the boil quickly. Time the blanching from when the water returns to a rapid boil. It is helpful to set a pinger for the blanching operation to ensure that the timing is accurate. When the blanching time is up, transfer the vegetables at once to a large bowl of iced water to prevent them over-cooking and to chill them quickly. Drain the vegetables thoroughly and spread them out on absorbent kitchen paper: pat dry and pack. Even if you are blanching only a small amount of vegetables, it is worthwhile to invest in a blanching basket which enables you to transfer the blanched vegetables to the cold water. A collapsible basket is light and folds flat for easy storage. The same blanching water can be used for up to seven batches of vegetables.

The following chart shows the method of preparation, blanching and packaging for various vegetables; also useful serving hints.

Vegetables	Preparation	Blanching time	Packaging	Serving hints
Asparagus	Wash and trim, blanch, grade and tie in bundles.	Thin stems 2 minutes Thick stems 4 minutes	Rectangular polythene containers	Serve with melted butter or hollandaise sauce. Use the stalk trimmings for soup.
Artichokes Globe	Remove outer leaves, trim tops and wash well.	7-10 minutes Add lemon juice to the blanching water	Polythene bags	Serve as a starter with vinaigrette dressing.
Jerusalem	Peel, cook in boiling salted water then mash to a purée.		Polythene containers Foil trays	Use the purée as a basis for soup.
Aubergines	Peel, cut in 1 inch/ 2.5 cm. slices and blanch. Cool and pack in layers using foil dividers.	4 minutes	Foil trays	Use for made-up dishes—ratatouille or moussaka—or cook in oil or butter and serve as a vegetable.
Avocados	Peel, remove the stones and purée the pulp with a little lemon juice and seasoning.		Polythene containers. Cover the surface with freezer film to prevent discolouration	Use the purée to make soup, dips or savoury spreads.

Beans				
Broad	Pod and blanch.	3 minutes	Polythene bags	Serve with parsley sauce.
French	Top and tail, slice or leave whole.	3 minutes	Polythene bags	
Runner	Trim, slice thickly.	2 minutes	Polythene bags	
Beetroot	Use small ones, cook until tender. Cool, peel, slice or dice.	Boil 40-50 minutes	Polythene containers	Serve with white sauce.
Broccoli	Trim, wash in salted water. Cut into sprigs, blanch and drain well.	3-5 minutes depending on size	Polythene containers	Serve with a knob of butter and a sprinkling of black pepper or nutmeg.
Brussels sprouts	Peel, trim and wash. Grade, blanch, and drain.	3-5 minutes	Polythene bags or containers	Serve mixed with cooked chestnuts.
Cabbage	Wash, shred finely or cut into wedges. Blanch and drain well.	1½ or 4 minutes according to cut	Polythene bags or containers	Serve with a knob of butter and a sprinkling of nutmeg or caraway seeds.
Carrots	Trim. Peel or scrape and wash: slice or dice.	4 minutes	Polythene bags or containers	Use in casseroles, or serve as a vegetable with a knob of butter.
Cauliflower	Trim into small sprigs, wash and blanch in salted water, drain well.	3 minutes	Polythene bags or containers	Serve with a white or cheese sauce.
Celery	Trim, scrub and cut into 1 inch/2.5 cm. lengths. Blanch and drain.	3 minutes	Polythene containers	Use only for cooked dishes.
Celeriac	Wash, peel, slice, steam until almost tender.		Polythene containers	Serve braised.
Chestnuts	Wash, peel and blanch, or cook until tender and purée	1-2 minutes	Polythene containers	Serve whole chestnuts with Brussels sprouts. Use unsweetened purée for stuffings: sweetened purée for mousses, sweet fillings, soufflés.
Chicory	Remove outer leaves, add lemon juice to blanching water and drain.	2 minutes	Polythene bags	Use in cooked dishes, or serve as a vegetable with a white sauce.

Corn-on-the-cob	Trim off leaves and silks, wash, blanch, cool and dry. (Use only young cobs.)	4-8 minutes depending on size	Individually in freezer film, then in Polythene containers	Serve as a starter with melted butter and black pepper, or as a vegetable.
Courgettes	Wash, trim into $\frac{1}{4}$-$\frac{1}{2}$ inch/$\frac{1}{2}$-1 cm. slices. Blanch or sauté in butter.	1 minute	Polythene containers	Serve as a vegetable or use in made-up dishes—ratatouille.
Fennel	Trim, wash, cut into $\frac{1}{4}$-$\frac{1}{2}$ inch/$\frac{1}{2}$-1 cm. slices. Blanch and drain.	3 minutes	Polythene bags	Serve as a vegetable with a cheese sauce. Not suitable to serve raw.
Marrow	Use small young ones, peel, cut into 1 inch/2.5. cm. slices and remove seeds. Blanch.	3 minutes	Polythene bags	Serve as a vegetable with a sprinkling of black pepper.
Mushrooms	Use small button mushrooms, wash. Sauté whole in butter for 1 minute, or slice larger ones.		Polythene containers	Use in savoury dishes, or serve with grilled meat or poultry.
Onions	Peel, chop and blanch.	2 minutes	Double polythene bags	Use for all savoury dishes.
Parsnips	Trim, peel, slice or dice, blanch and drain.	2 minutes	Polythene bags	Serve as a vegetable. Delicious roasted with a joint of beef.
Peas	Shell, blanch and drain.	1 minute	Polythene bags	Add a sprig of mint and sugar to the cooking water, if liked.
Mange tout	Trim ends, blanch and drain.	2-3 minutes	Polythene bags. Open freeze to ensure free-flow packs	
Peppers	Wash, remove stems, pips and pith, cut in halves or strips, blanch and drain.	3 minutes	Polythene containers	Use in casseroles.
Potatoes **Chipped**	Prepare chips and part fry 2 minutes, cool.		Polythene bags	
New	Scrape, cook until just tender.		Polythene bags	Serve with melted butter and a sprinkling of chopped chives.

Spinach	Wash carefully, blanch, drain well and pack.	2 minutes	Polythene containers	Serve as a vegetable, or with poached eggs, or as a flan filling.
Tomatoes	Skin, simmer for 5 minutes, rub through sieve, pack.		Polythene containers	Use for flavouring soups, sauces, and all savoury dishes.
Turnips	Trim, peel and dice, blanch and drain.	3 minutes	Polythene bags	Use in casseroles, or serve as a vegetable.

Freezing vegetables in boiling bags: Not all bags suitable for the freezer can afterwards be placed in boiling water, but boiling bags made of light gauge high density polythene will withstand both the low temperature within the freezer cabinet and submersion in boiling water. Blanching is a slow process inside such bags, so it is better to blanch the vegetables first and then pack in the bags. Or pack un-blanched vegetables which will be fully cooked after about 20 minutes boiling, such as sliced and washed leeks. Add seasoning and a knob of butter to the contents of the bag before sealing. Pack a number of bags together in a carton or batching bag to prevent damage in the freezer and you can prepare a selection of vegetables defrosting and reheating all in one saucepan.

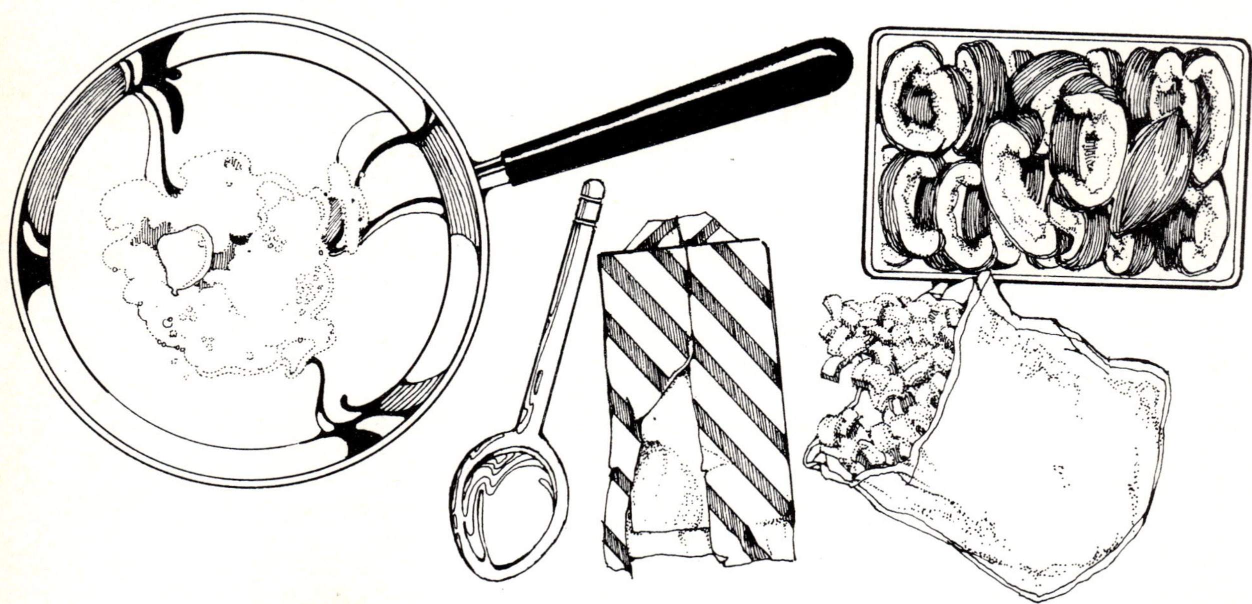

Freezing unblanched vegetables: When you are dealing with a glut crop of vegetables, or when you know that you are definitely going to be using the vegetables within a short period, certain ones may be frozen without blanching. They should be stored for not longer than 3 months. When cooking unblanched, frozen vegetables it is most important to give them the full cooking time. With blanched vegetables which have had some pre-cooking this is not necessary. Unblanched, frozen vegetables must be cooked from the freezer and not allowed to defrost as this may cause spoilage, due to the enzyme activity which has not been halted (as by blanching) and which will re-start in favourable conditions.

Carrots: Trim, scrape, wash and dry *young* carrots. Pack, whole, in polythene bags.

Cauliflower florets: Wash and dry small, tight florets and pack in polythene bags.

French beans: Top and tail the beans and leave them whole. Wash, drain well and pack in polythene bags. Unlike sliced green or runner beans, whole French beans have very few exposed cut surfaces and are therefore suitable for storage without blanching.

Mushrooms: Wash, dry and pack button mushrooms in polythene containers.

Onions: Pack chopped onions in double polythene bags to minimise the risk of any onion smell lingering in the freezer. It is useful to have chopped onion packed in small quantities for use when preparing casseroles, hot-pots and other savoury dishes.

Peppers: Wash, halve, remove the seeds and cores and slice the flesh. Pack in polythene containers.

Spinach: Wash, drain and pack tightly in polythene containers. Spinach is really better blanched, because of its bulk unblanched, when freezer space is at a premium.

Tomatoes: Wipe, remove the stem and freeze whole in polythene bags. Tomatoes frozen this way are suitable only for grilling or frying while still semi-frozen. They may be skinned under running water.

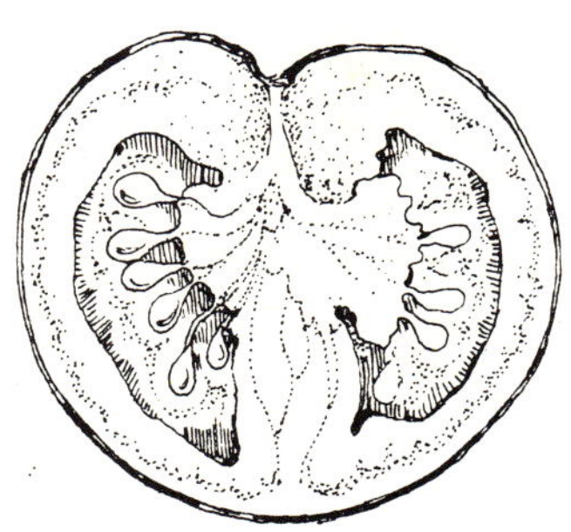

To cook frozen vegetables: Best results are obtained if blanched vegetables are cooked from the fozen state, or partially thawed. Cook them in the minimum salted water for half the usual time. They should not be mushy or soggy. Drain well and serve with a knob of butter. An alternative method of cooking frozen vegetables is to heat a knob of butter in a saucepan and add the partially thawed vegetables. Cook over a high heat for 1 minute to coat the vegetables with butter, then cover, lower the heat and cook until just tender, stirring from time to time. Add seasoning and serve.

Unusual tomato recipes: The glut of tomatoes sometimes results in providing more than a reasonable supply of tomato sauce, bagged tomatoes for cutting in half to grill or fry, and simple purées. Here are two more ways to exploit this delicious and prolific summer fruit.

Uncooked tomato chutney

Imperial/Metric
1½ lb/¾ kg. tomatoes
1 lb./450 g. onions, peeled
8 oz./225 g. sultanas
4 oz/100 g. sugar
1 tablespoon salt
1 tablespoon dry mustard
¼ teaspoon ground ginger
vinegar

American
1½ lb. tomatoes
1 lb. onions, peeled
1⅓ cups seedless white
    raisins
½ cup sugar
1 tablespoon salt
1 tablespoon dry mustard
¼ teaspoon ground ginger
vinegar

Mince the tomatoes and onions and place in a bowl. Add the sultanas, sugar, salt, mustard and ginger and mix all the ingredients thoroughly.
To freeze: Ladle into polythene containers and cover with cold vinegar. Seal and label the containers.
To use: Defrost at room temperature for about 45 minutes. To store in the larder or other cool place, ladle into a glass or stone jar and cover with the vinegar as above. Cover. (Out of the freezer the chutney will store for a limited period.)

Tomato curd

Imperial/Metric
1 lb./450 g. tomatoes
¼ pint/1½ dl. water
6 oz./175 g. sugar
3 oz./75 g. butter
finely grated zest and
    juice of 1 lemon
2 eggs

American
1 lb. tomatoes
⅔ cup water
¾ cup sugar
6 tablespoons butter
finely grated rind and
    juice of 1 lemon
2 eggs

Place the whole tomatoes in a pan with the water and simmer until the tomatoes are tender. Carefully drain off the liquid. Press the tomatoes through a nylon or hair sieve and place the purée in the top of a double boiler, or a bowl placed over a pan of boiling water. Add the sugar, butter, grated lemon zest and juice. Place over the heat until the sugar has thoroughly dissolved, stirring the mixture from time to time. Remove from the heat and allow the mixture to cool slightly, then add the eggs, well beaten. Return to the heat and cook until the curd has thickened.
To freeze: Cool slightly, then pour into polythene containers. Seal, label and store when cold.
To use: Defrost at room temperature for about 45 minutes. To store in the refrigerator (for up to 2 weeks) pour the curd into warmed jars, cover and seal.

Uncooked pickles and chutneys: These can be stored for long periods in the freezer. Do not store the preserve in untested glass jars, as they might fracture in the very low temperature inside the freezer cabinet. Instead use the polythene containers with snap-on seals. Remember to label the contents clearly and to leave a ½ inch/1 cm. headspace in the containers.

Freezing game: Keep game birds in insulated bags until ready to be prepared, then bleed and hang them, undrawn. It is essential to hang all game before freezing it as it needs to be cooked as soon as possible after defrosting. Feathered game may be frozen drawn and plucked or undrawn and with the feathers on. Its storage life in the freezer is limited when frozen undrawn and also game takes up more freezer space when frozen this way. Remember to keep the tail feathers from the pheasant if you want to use them to garnish the cooked dish.

Rabbit and hare: Joint and wipe the joints with a damp cloth. Wrap each joint in freezer film or foil, then place them together in one large polythene container or bag. The saddle from the hare may be packed separately for roasting and the joints packed as for rabbit.

Venison: This needs to be hung for 5-6 days to mature before being jointed and frozen. Venison benefits from being frozen in a marinade as it can be rather dry and tough.

Recording your freezer's contents

Even if you consider you have a good memory and the contents of your freezer are clearly labelled and well organised, it is still impossible to know at a moment's notice what you have in store. To save frustrating searches get into the habit of keeping a record of the stock in your freezer. It need not be an elaborate or expensive affair, or too complicated.

The simplest way to keep a freezer log is to have a small book with each page ruled into four columns. Head the columns as follows: date in, type of pack, number of packs, position. Indicate the number of packs by separate strokes which can be crossed through when a pack is taken from the freezer.

Another way of keeping a log is to use a card index system. A good way of keeping the contents of a chest freezer, in particular, on record is to purchase a magnetic board called The Freezer Finder. It has small metal strips on which you write and these are attached to the magnetised board, placing them in the corresponding positions to the packs in the freezer.

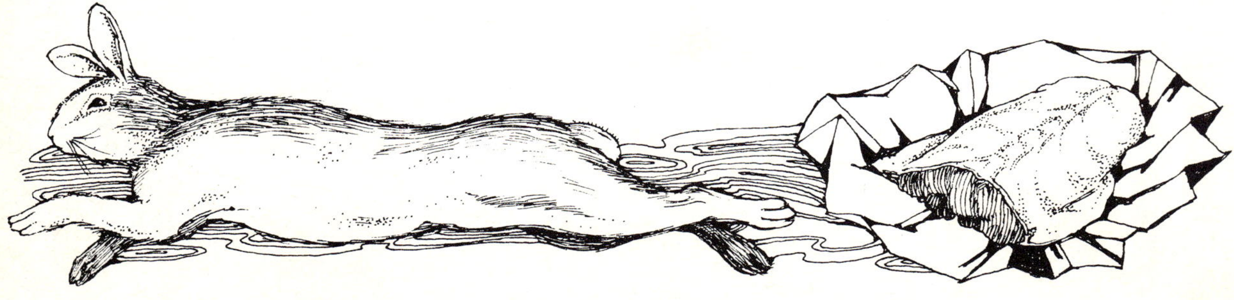

Autumn gardening hints

Early

Fruit
Harvest apples and pears. Store some fruit for eating purposes in a cool, airy room, preferably on slatted shelves. Turn some apples into a purée and freeze in polythene containers for use at a later date in made-up dishes. Prepare and freeze some made-up dishes using apples—pies, crumbles, flans, tarts. Harvest and freeze blackberries.

Vegetables
Continue to gather French and runner beans. Always pick them before they grow too large and become old and stringy. Prepare, blanch and freeze down beans which are in excess of your immediate requirements. Bring any tomatoes indoors now to allow them to ripen. Use as required or freeze as a purée for use in sauces and soups.

Plant out young spring cabbage plants raised from seed.

Mid-season

Fruit
Prune apple and pear trees.
Prune currant and gooseberry bushes.

Prepare the ground for planting fruit trees. Plant raspberries, blackberries and loganberries.

Vegetables
Winter lettuces are a worthwhile crop as they can be made into a delicious soup for the freezer.
An autumn sowing of broad beans can be made now providing you live in a part of the country with not too severe winters.
Start cropping Brussels sprouts by picking a few at a time from the bottom of each plant.

Lift Jerusalem artichokes. Prepare and freeze as a purée for making soup.

Sow a hardy, round-seeded pea such as Feltham First or Meteor.

Dig over the soil in the vegetable garden—providing the weather is suitable.

Late

Fruit
Spray fruit trees against pests such as aphids, suckers and winter moths. To encourage a good fruit crop next year dress fruit trees with a dressing of sulphate of potash.

Vegetables
Lift celery. This is good for making soup for the freezer and for blanching and freezing down.

Dig over and add garden compost or peat to the onion bed.

The trenches can be prepared for next year's runner beans.

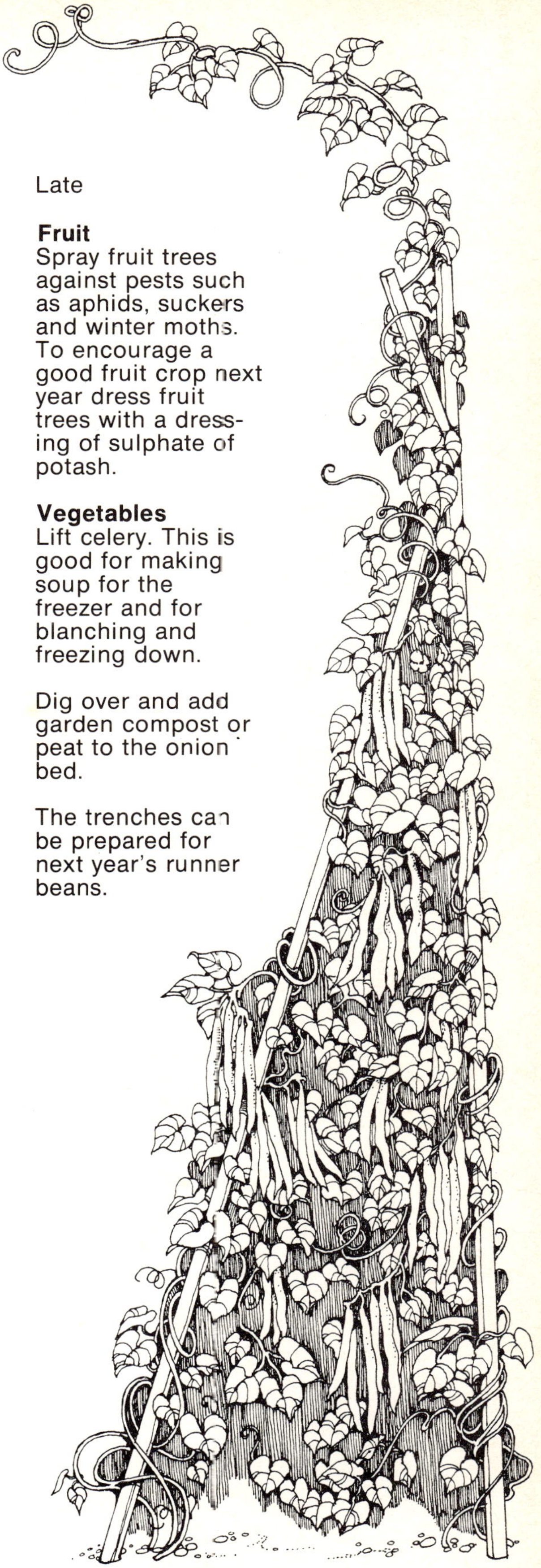

Candlelight buffet for eight people

This kind of informal gathering is so much more enjoyable than the unimaginative cocktail party, it is well worth the trouble of providing at least one hot dish for your guests.

Menu
Cold hors d'oeuvre — Cheddar
   mushroom caps, Scalloped eggs,
   Peanut dip
Quick tuna curry
Hawaiian pork cubes
Oven baked rice
Chocolate Viennese torte
Cardamon coffee
Fresh fruit

Place the Peanut dip in the centre of a large round tray and surround with cold finger hors d'oeuvre — olives, gherkins, pickled onions, carrot and celery sticks, Cheddar mushroom caps, Scalloped eggs, and potato crisps. Keep the Quick tuna curry, Hawaiian pork cubes and Baked rice hot on a warming tray or over candle warmers. If desired, serve hot garlic bread with the main course. Serve the Chocolate Viennese torte and Cardamon coffee from a small side table. For the centrepiece on the dessert table arrange grapes, clementines and fresh figs on glossy green leaves or a pedestal serving dish, and distribute lighted candles round the room.

Cheddar mushroom caps

Imperial/Metric
1 lb./450 g. button
  mushrooms
½ pint/2½ dl. chicken stock
2 oz./50 g. butter
3 oz./75 g. Cheddar cheese,
  grated
½ teaspoon Worcestershire
  sauce
pinch pepper
2 tablespoons chopped
  walnuts

American
1 lb. button mushrooms
1 cup chicken broth
¼ cup butter
¼ cup grated Cheddar
  cheese
½ teaspoon Worcestershire
  sauce
dash pepper
2 tablespoons chopped
  walnuts

Toss the mushrooms lightly in simmering stock for 3 minutes. Drain, and remove the stems. Beat together the butter, cheese, Worcestershire sauce and pepper. Pipe the cheese mixture into the mushroom cavities and sprinkle with chopped walnuts. Chill. To serve, spear on cocktail sticks.

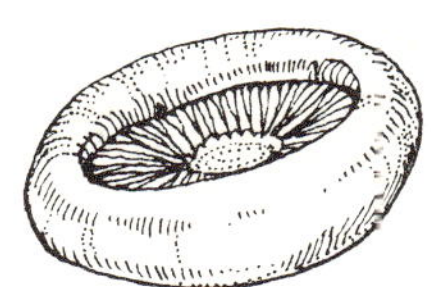

Scalloped eggs

Imperial/Metric
8 hard boiled eggs
2 tablespoons soured cream
1 teaspoon prepared
  mustard
salt and pepper
16 ½ inch/1 cm. ham cubes

American
8 hard cooked eggs
2 tablespoons soured cream
1 teaspoon prepared
  mustard
salt and pepper
16 ½ inch ham cubes

Cut the eggs in half crosswise and cut a thin slice off the base of each egg white half so they stand upright. Scoop out the yolk and mash with the soured cream and mustard. Season to taste with salt and pepper. Serrate the edges of the egg white halves and spoon the egg yolk filling into each half. Spear the ham cubes on cocktail sticks and spear through each filled egg half.

Peanut dip

Imperial/Metric
¼ pint/1½ dl. natural
  yogurt
¼ pint/1½ dl. cottage
  cheese
few drops Worcestershire
  sauce
pinch pepper
4 oz./125 g. peanuts

American
½ cup plain yogurt
½ cup creamed cottage
  cheese
dash Worcestershire sauce
dash pepper
1 cup peanuts

Blend the yogurt, cottage cheese, Worcestershire sauce and pepper until smooth. Coarsely chop the peanuts and stir into the yogurt mixture. Chill well before serving. Serve with potato crisps, savoury biscuits, celery and carrot sticks.

Quick tuna curry

Imperial/Metric
2 dessert apples
1 large onion
2 oz./50 g. butter
1 oz./25 g. plain flour
2-3 teaspoons curry
  powder
1 teaspoon salt
1½ pints/scant 1 litre
  milk
2 6½ oz./184 g. cans tuna
  fish
1 oz./25 g. flaked almonds

American
2 eating apples
1 large onion
¼ cup butter
¼ cup all-purpose flour
2-3 teaspoons curry
  powder
1 teaspoon salt
3¾ cups milk
2 6½ oz. cans tuna fish
¼ cup flaked almonds

Peel and finely chop the apples and onion. Sauté in the butter until soft. Stir in the flour, curry powder and salt and cook for 2-3 minutes. Gradually add the milk and cook until thickened, stirring constantly. Drain the tuna fish well and break into chunks. Add the tuna to the sauce and heat through. Toast the almonds in a moderate oven (350°F, 180°C, Gas Mark 4) until lightly browned. Sprinkle the toasted almonds over the tuna curry just before serving.

Hawaiian pork cubes

Imperial/Metric
1 lb./450 g. cooked lean
  pork
2 eggs
1 oz./25 g. plain flour
1 teaspoon salt
$\frac{1}{4}$ teaspoon pepper
fat for frying
4 sticks celery
2 tablespoons cooking oil
3 tablespoons cornflour
4 oz./125 g. white sugar
3 tablespoons soy sauce
$\frac{1}{4}$ pint/1$\frac{1}{2}$ dl. white vinegar
2 chicken stock cubes
$\frac{1}{2}$ pint/3 dl. hot water
8 oz./225 g. can pineapple
  pieces
freshly grated coconut
chopped parsley

American
1 lb. cooked lean pork
2 eggs
$\frac{1}{4}$ cup all-purpose flour
1 teaspoon salt
$\frac{1}{4}$ teaspoon pepper
fat for frying
4 stalks celery
2 tablespoons cooking oil
3 tablespoons cornstarch
$\frac{1}{2}$ cup granulated sugar
3 tablespoons soy sauce
$\frac{1}{2}$ cup white vinegar
2 chicken bouillon cubes
1$\frac{1}{4}$ cups hot water
8 oz. can pineapple chunks
freshly grated coconut
chopped parsley

Cut the cooked pork into 1 inch/2.5 cm. cubes. In a large bowl, beat together the eggs, flour, salt and pepper. Toss the pork cubes in the batter until coated. Fry the pork cubes in hot deep fat until crisp and brown. Drain well and keep warm. Slice the celery diagonally and sauté in the oil until just tender, about 10 minutes. Mix the cornflour with the sugar, soy sauce and vinegar. Dissolve the chicken stock cubes in the hot water and stir into the cornflour mixture. Pour the sauce over the celery and cook until thick, stirring constantly. Stir in the drained pineapple pieces and pork cubes. Heat through, stirring gently. Garnish with freshly grated coconut mixed with finely chopped parsley.

Oven baked rice

Imperial/Metric
1 lb./450 g. long grain rice
2 teaspoons salt
$\frac{1}{4}$ teaspoon white pepper
2 pints/generous 1 litre
  boiling water
8 lemon wedges
paprika pepper

American
2$\frac{2}{3}$ cups long grain rice
2 teaspoons salt
$\frac{1}{4}$ teaspoon pepper
5 cups boiling water
8 lemon wedges
paprika pepper

Put the rice, salt and pepper into a lightly buttered ovenproof casserole. Pour the boiling water over the rice. Cover tightly and bake in a moderate oven (350°F, 180°C, Gas Mark 4) for 40-50 minutes. Dip the edge of each lemon wedge in paprika. Arrange the lemon wedges on the baked rice.

 Chocolate Viennese torte

Imperial/Metric
8 oz./225 g. butter
8 oz./225 g. castor sugar
5 eggs, beaten
8 oz./225 g. plain flour
¼ teaspoon ground nutmeg
1 teaspoon vanilla essence
filling:
6 oz./175 g. chocolate
   chips
4 oz./125 g. butter
2 tablespoons water
2 tablespoons Crème de
   Caçao
4 egg yolks
2 tablespoons icing sugar
2 oz./50 g. chopped nuts

American
1 cup butter
1 cup granulated sugar
5 eggs, beaten
2 cups cake flour
¼ teaspoon ground nutmeg
1 teaspoon vanilla extract
filling:
1 cup chocolate chips
½ cup butter
2 tablespoons water
2 tablespoons Crème de
   Caçao
4 egg yolks
2 tablespoons
   confectioner's sugar
½ cup chopped nuts

First make the cake. Cream the butter and sugar together until light and fluffy. Gradually add the eggs and beat with an electric mixer for about 10 minutes. Fold in the flour, spice and vanilla essence. Pour into a greased 2 lb./1 kg. loaf tin and bake in a moderate oven (325°F, 170°C, Gas Mark 3) for 1¼ hours. Turn out and cool on a wire rack. Meanwhile, combine the chocolate chips, butter, water and Crème de Caçao in a heavy saucepan and heat until blended. Cool to lukewarm. Lightly beat the egg yolks with the sugar and stir into the chocolate mixture. Chill for 1 hour, then beat until spreading consistency. Slice the cake horizontally into 6 layers. Spread the chocolate icing between each layer and on the top and sides of the cake. Sprinkle the chopped nuts on the top of the cake. Chill several hours before serving.

 Cardamon coffee

Imperial/Metric
2½ pints/1½ litres boiling
   water
4 tablespoons instant
   coffee granules
1 teaspoon ground
   cardamon
¼ pint/1½ dl. double cream

American
6 cups boiling water
4 tablespoons instant
   coffee granules
1 teaspoon ground
   cardamon
½ cup whipping cream

Pour the boiling water over the instant coffee and cardamon. Pour into coffee cups and spoon lightly whipped double cream on top.

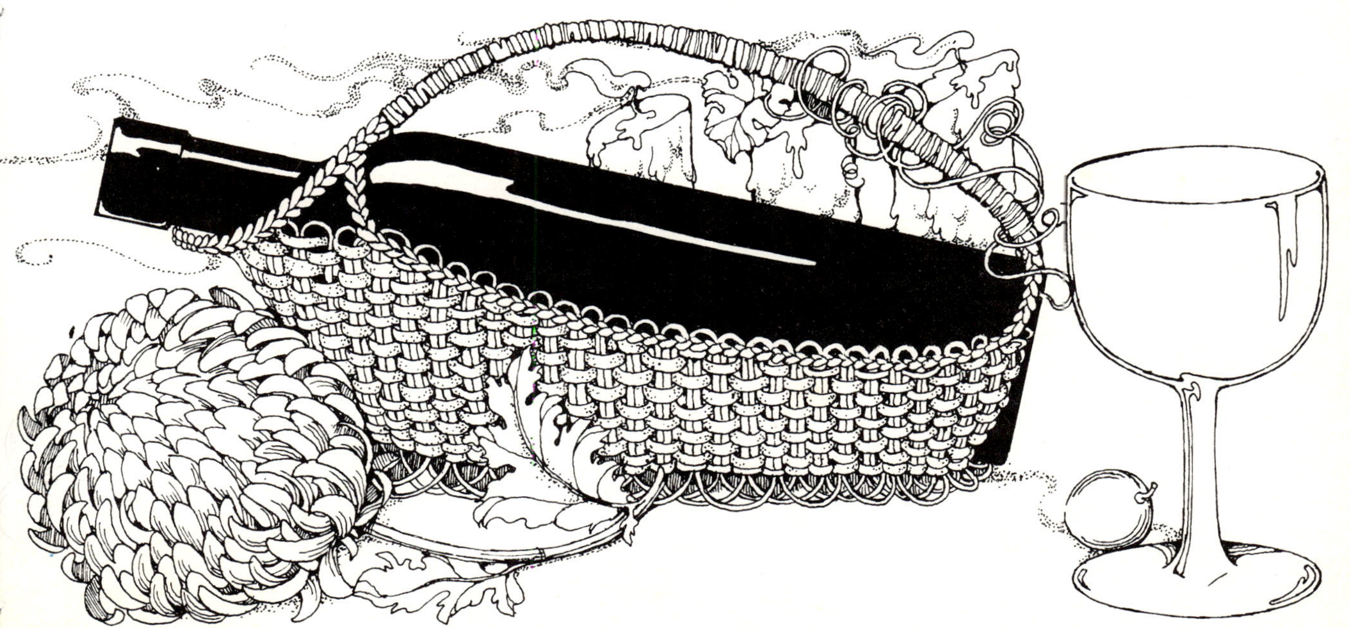